AIRCREW
SURVIVAL

AIRCREW SURVIVAL

DEPARTMENT OF THE AIR FORCE

AF PAMPHLET 64-5

BARNES
&NOBLE
BOOKS
NEW YORK

1996 Barnes & Noble Books

ISBN 0-76070-183-0

Printed and bound in the United States of America

M 9 8 7 6 5 4 3 2 1

RRDH

Search and Rescue

Aircrew Survival

This pamphlet is designed to aid your survival and rescue efforts regardless of geographic location or climatic condition. It describes, in outline form, the basic survival skills which you have learned. It will assist you in recognizing and using the natural resources at hand. This information plus your will to survive are necessary to ensure your survival.

Supersedes AFM 64-5, 15 August 1969. (See signature page for summary of changes.)
No. of Printed Pages: 122
OPR: HQ ATC/DONZ (MSgt R. Paetz)
Approved by: HQ ATC/DON (Col W. W. Miller)
Editor: R. E. Penoff
Distribution: F

Page

Attachment

Chapter 1

COMBAT SURVIVAL CHECKLIST

> SOUND AND DELIBERATE DECISIONS ARE THE KEYS
> TO COMBAT SURVIVAL, REMEMBER, YOU'RE IN SHOCK!!

1-1. After Landing:

a. Take action necessary for protection in a nuclear, biological, and chemical (NBC) environment (if applicable).

b. Assess medical problems.

c. Assume enemy presence and take cover.

d. Apply personal camouflage, disguise body odor.

e. Depending on the situation, retain or discard specific equipment. If discarding, hide it. Remember that some of your items can be used for camouflage.

f. Move to a hole-up site (away from enemy positions and landing site)!!

NOTE: A spiritual survival checklist is in attachment 1.

1-2. Moving to a Hole-Up Site:

a. Do not leave evidence of travel.

b. Use zigzagging movement techniques.

c. Use terrain masking wisely. Remember, terrain that is hard for you to travel in is also hard for the enemy.

d. Stay away from lines of communication (roads, rivers, railroads, trails) and people.

e. Travel slowly and deliberately.

f. Be alert for enemy activity.

g. Use shadows for concealment.

h. Use effective light and noise discipline.

1-3. Selecting a Hole-Up Site. Select a site that provides:

a. Adequate concealment.

b. An observation point.

c. Avenues for escape.

d. Protection from the environment.

e. For possible radio/visual communications opportunities.

1-4. Actions to Accomplish at a Hole-Up Site. This will be the best time to study this checklist.

a. Be alert!

b. Provide for personal protection.

c. Treat injuries.

d. Restore body fluids (drink water).

e. Re-apply personal camouflage.

f. Be aware that body odor and body waste could compromise your position. Body odor should be disguised by rubbing dirt, plants, etc., over your body.

g. Evaluate combat survival problems.

h. Determine general or specific position.

i. Inventory your equipment.

j. Determine or review your plan of action.

k. Plan for and take care of water and food requirements.

l. Mentally prepare for long-term survival.

m. Determine travel times and routes.

n. Evaluate recovery possibilities.

o. Follow established communication procedures.

p. Improvise needed equipment.

1-5. Movement and Travel Considerations:

a. Physical condition.

b. Location and destination.

c. Distance from battle areas.

d. Enemy presence.

e. Environment.

f. Terrain and distance that must be covered.

g. Food and water requirements.

1-6. Movement and Travel Techniques:

a. STOP - LOOK - LISTEN.

b. Travel slowly and deliberately.

c. Leave no evidence of travel.

d. Avoid open areas and lines of communication.

e. Observe for other movement.

f. Utilize available cover.

g. Use shadows for concealment.

h. Avoid skylining.

i. Avoid being spotted from the air.

j. Use terrain-masking techniques.

k. Avoid domestic animals.

l. Select concealed rest areas which provide an observation point.

m. Maintain desired direction of travel.

1-7. Recovery Site Selection:

a. Areas that are within search and rescue (SAR) range.

b. Select sites free of hazards.

c. Select landing sites for helicopter recovery.

d. Select areas according to premission briefing.

e. Select sites that optimize conditions for radio communications and use of signaling devices.

f. Use terrain masking to protect from enemy threats.

1-8. SAR Communication Procedures:

a. Transmit in the "blind" only if briefed, or as a last resort.

b. Communicate as briefed.

c. Remember that communication or signaling devices could compromise your position.

Chapter 2

EVADING THE ENEMY

2-1. Planning:
   a. Evasion - the responsibility of every fighting man (figure 2-1).

U.S. FIGHTING MAN'S
CODE OF CONDUCT

I
   I am an American fighting man. I serve in the forces which guard my country and our way of life. I am prepared to give my life in their defense.

II
   I will never surrender of my own free will. If in command, I will never surrender my men while they still have the means to resist.

Figure 2-1. Code of Conduct.

   b. Where to go:
      (1) An area for immediate pickup.
      (2) A *safe* area or as briefed in premission intelligence briefings.
      (3) A front-line area, if recommended in the premission briefing.
      (4) To a neutral or friendly country or area.

   c. Guidelines for successful evasion:
      (1) Have a "can do" attitude.
      (2) Use established procedures.
      (3) Have a definite plan of action and set attainable goals.
      (4) Observe rules of camouflage, concealment, and movement.
      (5) Be patient.
      (6) Conserve food, but never pass up a chance to obtain food if it can be done safely.
      (7) Conserve strength for critical periods.

(8) Rest and sleep as much as possible.

(9) Stay out of sight of all people.

2-2. Camouflage:

a. Three rules:

(1) Disturb the area as little as possible.

(2) Avoid activity which reveals movement to the enemy.

(3) Apply camouflage.

Figure 2-2. Natural Concealment.

b. Common sense:

(1) Take advantage of all natural concealment (figure 2-2).

(2) Don't over camouflage; too much is as obvious as too little.

(3) When using natural camouflage, remember that foliage fades and wilts; change it regularly.

(4) If taking advantage of shadows and shade, remember, they shift with the sun (figure 2-3).

(5) Avoid unnecessary movement.

Figure 2-3. Shadows.

(6) When moving, avoid skyline (figure 2-4).

(7) Never expose anything that may shine (for example, watch, glasses, pen, and pencils) (figure 2-5).

(8) Break up the outline of the body (figure 2-6).

(9) When observing an area, do so from a prone position and concealment (figure 2-7).

c. Blend with the local environment by applying:
   (1) Vegetation.
   (2) Stains from grasses, berries, dirt, and charcoal.

d. Use camouflage patterns (figure 2-8).
   (1) Blotch pattern (figure 2-8):

Figure 2-4. Avoid Skyline.

    (a) Temperate deciduous (leaf shedding) areas—blotch method.
    (b) Desert areas (barren)—blotch method.
    (c) Barren snow—blotch method.
  (2) Slash pattern (figure 2-8):
    (a) Coniferous (evergreen) areas—broad slash method.
    (b) Jungle areas—broad slash method.
    (c) Grass—slash method.

  e. Camouflage application:
  (1) Face. Use darker colors on high spots and lighter colors on the remaining exposed areas (mask, netting, or flop hat may help).
  (2) Ears. The insides and the backs should have two colors to break up outlines.
  (3) Head and neck (often forgotten). Use scarf, collar, vegetation, netting, or coloration methods.

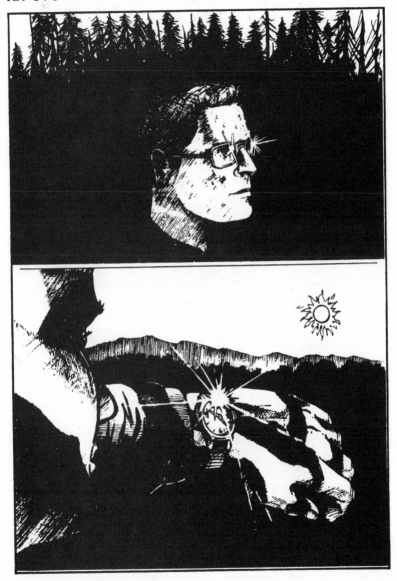

Figure 2-5. Avoiding Shine.

Figure 2-6. Breaking Up Outline.

Figure 2-7. Observation.

BLOTCH   **SLASH**

Figure 2-8. Camouflage Patterns.

   (4) Hands. Backs of wrists and between fingers (gloves or mittens).

   (5) Body. Break up the "V" of the crotch and armpits.

   (6) Odors stand out and may give an evader away. Do not use:

      (a) Scented soaps and shampoos.

      (b) Shaving cream, after shave lotion, or other cosmetics.

      (c) Insect repellant—camouflage stick is least scented; some local plant juices may work.

      (d) Gum and candy, they have strong or sweet smells.

      (e) Tobacco—the odor is unmistakable.

2-3. Shelter for Resting or Sleeping:

   a. Full use must be made of concealment and camouflage.

   b. Locate carefully:

   (1) Choose area least likely to be searched (drainages, rough terrain, etc.).

(2) One that affords best escape routes. Have observable approaches when possible. Don't corner yourself.

(3) Least obvious location—looks like everything else.

(4) Concealment with minimum to no preparation (figure 2-9).

(5) Select natural concealment area.

(6) Avoid staying in one area too long.

(7) Entrances and exits should be located in brush and along ridges, ditches, and rocks to keep from forming paths to site.

(8) Ensure overhead concealment.

c. Easy to remember acronym:

B	-	**B**lend.
L	-	**L**ow silhouette.
I	-	**I**rregular shape.
S	-	**S**mall.
S	-	**S**ecluded location.

Figure 2-9. Natural Shelters.

Figure 2-10. Ground Movement.

2-4. Movement:

a. Movement at the wrong time will pinpoint an evader's location quicker than any other evasion factors. A moving object is much easier to spot. If travel is necessary, then movement should be:

(1) Masked by natural cover (figure 2-10).

(2) Restricted to periods of limited light, foul weather, wind, or when enemy activity is lightest (figure 2-11).

Figure 2-11. Travel Restriction.

(3) Sporadic - every five to ten paces the evader should:

(a) STOP at a point of concealment.

(b) LOOK for signs of human or animal activity; that is, smoke, tracks, roads, troops, vehicles, aircraft, wire, buildings, etc. Peripheral vision may be more effective for recognizing movement at night and twilight.

(c) LISTEN for vehicles, troops, aircraft, weapons, animals.

(4) Quiet, be aware of the sound of clothing (brushing) when moving.

b. An important factor is to break up the human shape or lines that are recognizable at a long distance.

c. Selecting routes of travel requires detailed planning and the use of special techniques (such as, irregular travel route or zigzag) to camouflage evidence of travel.

d. Some techniques of limiting or concealing evidence of travel are:
(1) Avoid disturbing the vegetation above knee level.
(a) Don't break branches, leaves, or grass.
(b) Use a walking stick to part vegetation and push it back to its original position.
(c) Don't grab small trees or brush, this may scruff the bark at eye level and can be spotted from a distance. In snow country, this may mark a path of snowless vegetation that can be spotted.
(2) Pick firm footing carefully and place the foot lightly, but squarely on the surface to avoid:
(a) Overturning ground cover, rocks, and sticks.

Figure 2-12. Travel Concealment.

(b) Scuffing bark on logs and sticks.

(c) Making noise by breaking sticks (cloth wrapped around feet helps muffle this).

(d) Slipping.

(e) Mangling of low grass and bushes that would normally spring back.

(3) When tracks are unavoidable in soft footing, mask your tracks by:

(a) Placing track in the shadows of vegetation, downed logs, and snowdrifts (figure 2-12).

(b) Moving before and during precipitation will allow tracks to fill in.

(c) Traveling during windy periods.

(d) Taking advantage of solid surfaces (logs, rocks, etc.) which leave no evidence of travel.

(e) Brushing or patting out tracks lightly to speed their breakdown or make them look old (figure 2-13).

Figure 2-13. Removing Travel Evidence.

(4) Don't litter. Trash or equipment will often identify who dropped or lost it. Secure everything so that it is not lost and hide or bury anything to be discarded.

  e. Obstacle penetration:
    (1) Go around chain-link and wire fences if possible.
    (2) Penetrate rail fences by going under or between lower rails. If impractical, go over the top, presenting as low a silhouette as possible (figure 2-14).

Figure 2-14. Rail Fences.

    (3) Roads should be crossed after observation from concealment to determine enemy activity. Cross at points offering best cover such as bushes, shadows, bend in road, etc. (figure 2-15).
    (4) Railroad tracks should be observed in the same manner as roads. Then align body parallel to tracks and face down, cross tracks, using a semipushup motion; repeat for second track (figure 2-16).

Figure 2-15. Road Crossing.

Figure 2-16. Railroad Tracks.

(5) Deep ditches should be entered feet first to avoid injury. Watch for trip wires and booby traps. Avoid leaving evidence of travel (figure 2-17).

Figure 2-17. Deep Ditches.

Chapter 3

MEDICAL

3-1. Survival Medical Problems:

a. When breathing stops:

(1) If a victim appears to be unconscious, shake the victim and shout.

(2) If there is no response:

(a) Tilt the victim's head, chin pointing up.

(b) Immediately look, listen, and feel for air.

(3) If the victim is not breathing:

(a) Give four quick breaths:

1. If no air exchange, reposition head and try again.

2. If no air exchange:

a. Turn victim on side and give four back blows between shoulder blades.

b. Turn victim on back and give four abdominal thrusts.

c. Check mouth for obstruction.

(b) If there is still no breathing, begin rate of one breath every 5 seconds.

b. Control bleeding:

(1) Apply a direct pressure dressing and elevate. (If this doesn't work, apply a tighter dressing over the first one.)

(2) Use pressure points to control bleeding (6 to 10 minutes) (figure 3-1).

(3) Use a tourniquet only after every alternate method has been attempted. If unable to get to medical aid within 2 hours, after 20 minutes, gradually loosen the tourniquet. If bleeding has stopped, remove tourniquet; if bleeding continues, reapply and leave in place.

c. Fractures, sprains, and dislocations:

(1) Treat wounds:

(a) Stop bleeding.

(b) Apply dry, clean dressing.

(2) Place in a position of function.

(3) Splint (immobilizing joints above and below injury).

(4) Apply cold to control swelling (apply heat after 48 hours).

(5) Check periodically to assure circulation.

d. Shock (treat for all injuries):

(1) Treat injury.

(2) Prevent loss of body heat.

(3) Elevate the lower extremities if the injury will not be aggravated and if there are no abdominal or head injuries.

(4) Do not give liquids to unconscious victim.

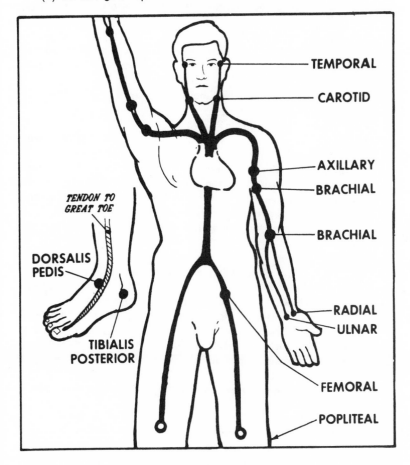

Figure 3-1. Pressure Points.

3-2. Common Survival Injuries and Illnesses:

  a. Burns:

    (1) Cool as rapidly as possible.

    (2) Leave objects (cloth, dirt, etc.) in burn area; they are sterile.

    (3) Apply a dry, clean dressing.

    (4) Drink water with salt if possible (¼ teaspoon per quart).

    (5) Change dressings as needed to prevent infection.

  b. Eye injuries:

    (1) Sun blindness (gritty, burning sensation, and possible reduction of vision; may be caused by reflection from sun on snow, water, sand, etc.):

      (a) Cover both eyes with moist bandage if it won't cause cold injury (or a dry sterile bandage).

      (b) Leave bandage on for 18 hours.

      (c) Victim extremely susceptible to future occurrences.

    (2) Foreign objects in eyes:

      (a) Irrigate with clean water.

      (b) An improvised cotton swab, using gentle swipes over affected area, may remove stubborn particles.

      (c) If unsuccessful, apply eye ointment, if available.

      (d) Patch eyes for 24 hours.

  c. Heat disorders:

    (1) Heat cramps (cramps in legs or abdomen):

      (a) Rest.

      (b) Drink water with salt added (¼ teaspoon per quart).

    (2) Heat exhaustion (pale; heavy sweating; moist, cool skin).

      (a) Rest in shade.

      (b) Drink water with salt added (¼ teaspoon per quart).

    (3) Heat stroke (skin hot and dry; no sweating; fast, strong pulse), IMPORTANT - *handle gently:*

      (a) Cool as rapidly as possible (saturate clothing with water and fan).

      (b) Do not give stimulants.

      (c) Avoid overcooling.

  d. Cold injuries:

    (1) Frostbite (freezing of body tissue):

      (a) Superficial frostbite (only skin tissue is affected):

        1. Will appear as grayish or yellow-white spot on the skin; feels numb.

        2. May be rewarmed using body heat (crotch, armpits, buddy's abdomen).

        3. May be rewarmed using warm water. (Water should be comfortably warm to a normally protected part of the body such as the elbow.)

        4. *Do Not Rub Frozen Tissue.*

        5. *Do Not Thaw by Using Fire.*

    (b) Deep frostbite (frozen to the bone):

        1. Stiff, numb, blue.

        2. Leave frozen; prevent further freezing and damage. (If thawing is promoted, victim will probably experience severe pain and may become incapacitated.)

    (2) Hypothermia (lowering of the body core temperature), IMPORTANT - *handle gently:*

      (a) Warm as rapidly as possible.

        1. Insulate against further heat loss to include the head.

        2. Skin-to-skin contact (two buddies in a sleeping bag).

        3. Drink warm fluids.

        4. Eat foods high in carbohydrates.

      (b) Put on dry clothing, if available.

  e. Skin tissue damage:

    (1) Immersion injuries:

      (a) Resemble dishpan hands.

      (b) Avoid walking while feet are affected.

      (c) Pat dry; don't rub; skin tissue will be sensitive.

      (d) Dry socks and shoes (keep feet protected).

      (e) Assure circulation is not impaired (tight boots, cuffs, etc.).

    (2) Saltwater sores:

      (a) Keep sores dry.

      (b) Do not open or squeeze sores.

      (c) Use antiseptic, if available.

  f. Injected toxins:

    (1) Snakebite:

      (a) Nonpoisonous snakebite. Clean and bandage wound.

      (b) Poisonous snakebite (figure 3-2). IMPORTANT: If the victim shows signs of envenomation (swelling, intense pain), and there will be a delay of more than 4 to 5 hours before a hospital can be reached, incision and suction will be needed. This should be done within the first 30 minutes and only on an extremity.

    (2) Marine life:

        (a) Flush wound with water.

        (b) Allow wound to bleed freely temporarily.

        (c) For stings, place affected part in hot water, or apply hot compresses for 30 to 60 minutes (as hot as victim can tolerate).

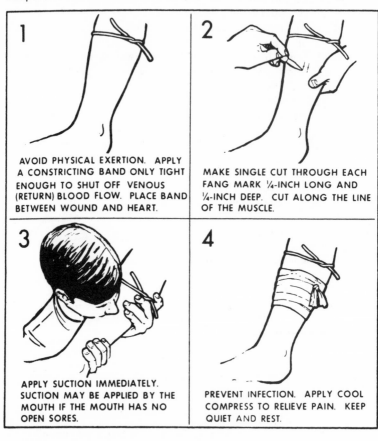

1 AVOID PHYSICAL EXERTION. APPLY A CONSTRICTING BAND ONLY TIGHT ENOUGH TO SHUT OFF VENOUS (RETURN) BLOOD FLOW. PLACE BAND BETWEEN WOUND AND HEART.

2 MAKE SINGLE CUT THROUGH EACH FANG MARK ¼-INCH LONG AND ¼-INCH DEEP. CUT ALONG THE LINE OF THE MUSCLE.

3 APPLY SUCTION IMMEDIATELY. SUCTION MAY BE APPLIED BY THE MOUTH IF THE MOUTH HAS NO OPEN SORES.

4 PREVENT INFECTION. APPLY COOL COMPRESS TO RELIEVE PAIN. KEEP QUIET AND REST.

Figure 3-2. Snakebite Treatment.

     (d) Cover wound with clean dressing.

     (e) Treatment for shock and (or) artificial respiration may be required.

  g. Ingested toxins:

    (1) Stay quiet and lie down.

    (2) Drink large amounts of water.

    (3) Do *not* induce vomiting if:

     (a) Victim is unconscious.

     (b) Obvious burns appear on the lips or in the throat.

     (c) Poison is petroleum based product.

  h. Surface toxins:

    (1) Wash with large amounts of water and soap, if available.

    (2) Keep covered to prevent scratching.

  i. Infection:

    (1) Keep clean.

    (2) Iodine tablet solution can be used.

    (3) Change bandages as needed.

  j. Cold, flu, etc. Drink water, eat, rest, and keep warm and dry.

  k. Dysentery; diarrhea:

    (1) Drink water, liquid diet.

    (2) Consuming charcoal, charred bone, or chalk made into a paste will act as a regulator.

  l. Constipation:

    (1) Normal.

    (2) Don't take laxatives.

    (3) Exercise.

    (4) Drink water.

  m. Scurvy (bleeding from gums, loosening of teeth, swelling in joints, wounds won't heal):

    (1) Lack of vitamin C.

    (2) Eat raw greens, fruit, evergreen tea (boil evergreen needles for 5 minutes and discard needles).

  n. Beriberi (muscle cramps and (or) twitching in legs, loss of appetite, paralysis):

    (1) Lack of vitamin B.

    (2) Eat any green foods; bark tea (boil outer layer for 5 minutes and discard bark).

o. Protein deficiency (irritability, loss of appetite, vomiting, diarrhea, muscular wasting, fluid retention):

(1) Eat meat, insects, and eggs.

(2) Eat grains and nuts.

3-3. Sanitation and Hygiene:

a. Stay clean:

(1) Washing minimizes the chance of infection.

(2) White ashes, sand, or loamy soil can be used as soap substitutes.

(3) Short periods of exposure to sunshine and open air will help refresh the body.

b. Lice, fleas, ticks, bedbugs, etc:

(1) Pick off and crush (including eggs).

(2) Wash clothing.

(3) Check body regularly.

(4) Clean skin to prevent infection.

(5) Use smoke fire to fumigate clothing and equipment.

c. Hair:

(1) Hair should be kept trimmed and face should be clean shaven, if possible, to prevent parasites and bacterial growth.

(2) If unable to shave or trim hair, comb regularly.

d. Mouth and teeth:

(1) Brush at least daily. If no toothbrush is available, a hardwood twig, once washed, can be frayed by chewing on one end.

(2) Single strands of inner core from suspension line can be used for dental floss.

(3) Gum tissues should be stimulated by rubbing with a clean finger.

(4) Gargling with a salt and water solution may help prevent sore throats as well as aid in cleaning teeth and gums.

e. Feet:

(1) Feet should be washed, dried, and massaged daily.

(2) Shoes should have sufficient room to prevent pressure spots, but not allow sliding while walking.

(3) Socks should be changed or washed daily. Repair promptly.

(4) Check feet frequently for blisters and red spots. Adhesive tape may help prevent further damage.

   f. Clothing:

     (1) Avoid getting dirty.

     (2) Clothing should be washed if dirty.

     (3) Bacteria and mildew may be destroyed by hanging in sunny air.

   g. Rest:

     (1) Regular rest periods should be included in daily activities.

     (2) Learn to rest under less-than-ideal conditions.

3-4. Rules for Avoiding Illness:

   a. All water obtained from natural sources should be purified.

   b. Use "cat holes" to keep waste away from camp.

   c. Wash hands before preparing food or water and after handling any disease-carrying material.

   d. All eating utensils should be cleaned after each meal.

   e. Clean the mouth and teeth thoroughly at least once each day.

   f. Insects and insect bites can be prevented by properly using repellent (unless evading), equipment (head net), and clothing.

   g. Dry any wet clothing as soon as possible.

   h. If possible, get 7 or 8 hours of sleep per night.

Chapter 4

PERSONAL PROTECTION

4-1. Use and Care of Clothing:

a. The acronym COLDER can be used to remember how to use and care for clothing.

> **C** - Keep clothing **C**lean
> **O** - Avoid **O**verheating
> **L** - Wear clothing **L**oose and in **L**ayers
> **D** - Keep clothing **D**ry
> **E** - **E**xamine clothing for defects or wear
> **R** - Keep clothing **R**epaired

b. Keep clothing clean since dirt reduces its insulative qualities.
(1) Do not sit or lie directly on the ground.
(2) Wash clothing whenever possible.

c. To avoid overheating:
(1) Remove layers of clothing during any stenuous activities.
(2) When fully clothed, the majority of the body's heat escapes through the head and neck areas:
(a) Use a hat to regulate body heat.
(b) In hot environments, the hat should be kept on whenever in direct sunlight.
(3) On the ocean in hot weather, wet down clothing.
(a) Use salt water, not drinking water.
(b) Dry clothing before dark to prevent hypothermia.

d. Wear clothing loose and layered (figure 4-1).
(1) Tight clothing restricts blood flow which regulates body temperature.
(2) Layers create more dead air space.
(3) In hot areas keep entire body covered to prevent sunburn and dehydration.

e. Keep clothing dry to maintain its insulative qualities.
(1) Damp clothing may be dried quickly in the sun or by a fire.
(2) If you fall into the water in the winter:
(a) Roll in powdery snow to blot up moisture.
(b) Brush off snow and roll again until most of the water is absorbed.

Figure 4-1. Sun Protection.

(c) Finish drying by a fire.

(3) If no fire is available:
   (a) Remove clothing and get into sleeping bag (if available).
   (b) Allow wet clothes to freeze.
   (c) Break ice out of clothing.

f. Examine clothing frequently for any damage, and repair when necessary using:

(1) Needle and thread with parachute material patches (figure 4-2).

(2) Safety pins.
(3) Tape.
(4) Improvised foot protection (figures 4-3, 4-4, and 4-5).

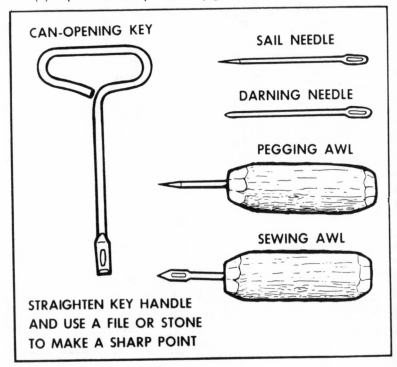

Figure 4-2. Improvised Needles.

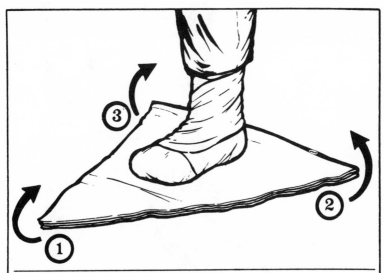

1. CUT TWO TO FOUR LAYERS OF PARACHUTE CLOTH INTO A 30—INCH SQUARE
2. FOLD INTO A TRIANGLE
3. PLACE FOOT ON TRIANGLE WITH TOES POINTING TOWARD CORNER
4. FOLD FRONT OVER THE TOES
5. FOLD SIDE CORNERS, ONE AT A TIME, OVER THE INSTEP

Figure 4-3. Hudson Bay Duffel.

4-2. Shelters:

a. Site selection:
 (1) Near signal and recovery site.
 (2) Food and water available.
 (3) Avoid natural hazards:
  (a) Dead standing trees.
  (b) Drainages and dry river beds except in combat areas.
  (c) Avalanche areas.

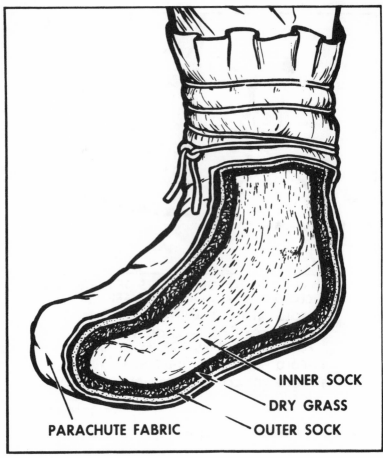

INNER SOCK

DRY GRASS

PARACHUTE FABRIC   **OUTER SOCK**

Figure 4-4. Double Sock.

    (4) Location large and level enough to lie down in.

    (5) Close to building materials.

   b. Types of shelters:

    (1) In any weather, immediate shelter may be found which requires minimal improvements (figures 4-6 and 4-7).

    (2) In most temperate climates, protection from wind and rain is sufficient (figure 4-8).

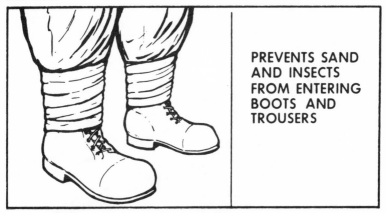

PREVENTS SAND
AND INSECTS
FROM ENTERING
BOOTS AND
TROUSERS

Figure 4-5. Gaiters.

Figure 4-6. Desert Shelters.

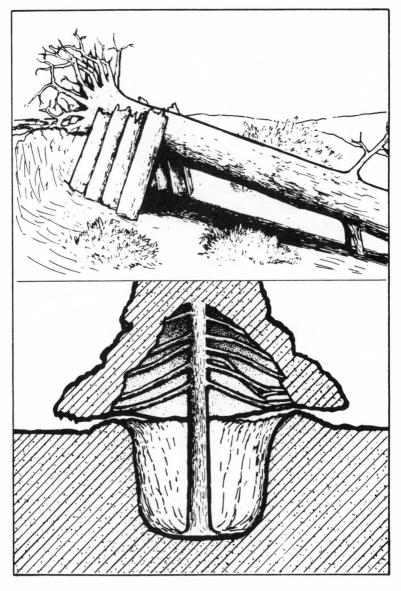

Figure 4-7. Immediate Action Shelters.

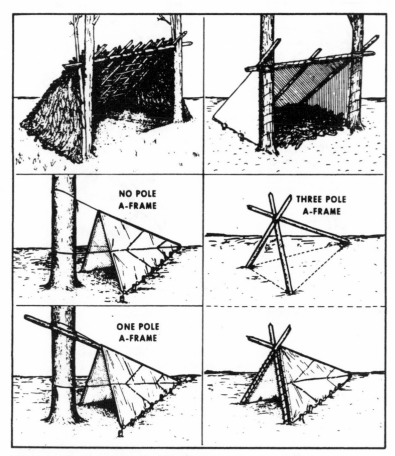

Figure 4-8. Temperate Shelters.

(3) In cold climates, an enclosed, insulated shelter will be required. Snow will be the most abundant insulating material (figures 4-9, 4-10, 4-11, and 4-12). An air vent is required to prevent carbon monoxide poisoning when using an open flame inside enclosed shelters.

NOTE: As a general rule, unless you can see your breath - your snow shelter is too warm and should be cooled down to preclude melting and dripping.

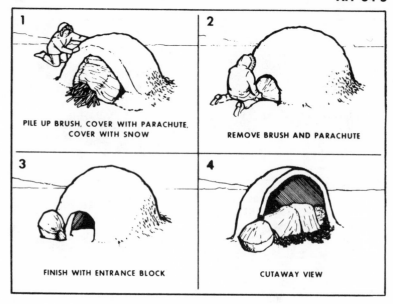

Figure 4-9. Molded Dome.

(4) A shade shelter will be required in hot climates.

(a) The shelter floor should be elevated or dug down (approximately 18 inches) to reduce the surface temperature.

(b) For maximum protection, a minimum of two layers of parachute material suspended 12-18 inches above the head is required. White is the best color to reflect heat (figure 4-13); inner-most layer should be of darker material.

(5) In wet climates, an enclosed, elevated shelter is needed for protection from dampness and insects (figure 4-14).

c. Shelter construction materials:
(1) Raft and raft parts.
(2) Aircraft parts.
(3) Parachute material.
(4) Sheet of plastic or plastic bag.
(5) Bark peeled off dead trees.
(6) Boughs and broad leaves.

Figure 4-10. Snow Cave.

    (7) Grass and sod.
    (8) Snow.
    (9) Sand and rocks.

  d. Shelter construction:
    (1) Have entrance 90° to prevailing wind (figure 4-15).

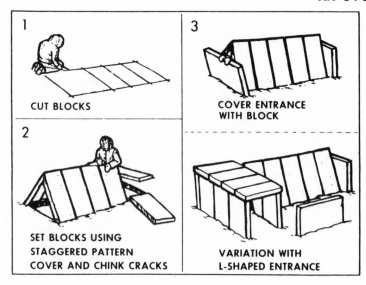

Figure 4-11. Fighter Trench.

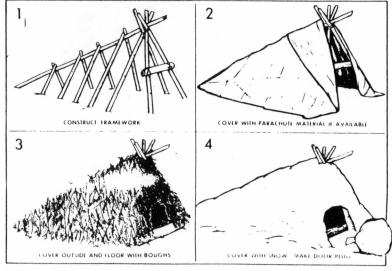

Figure 4-12. Thermal A-Frame.

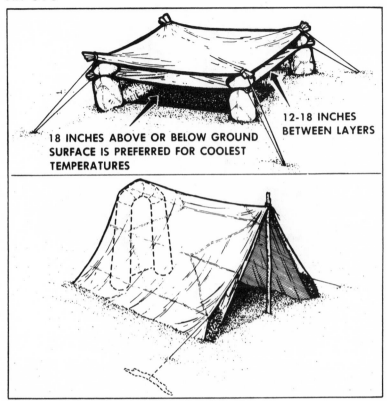

12-18 INCHES BETWEEN LAYERS

18 INCHES ABOVE OR BELOW GROUND SURFACE IS PREFERRED FOR COOLEST TEMPERATURES

Figure 4-13. Shade Shelters.

(2) The framework can be constructed from poles, rocks, suspension line, etc.

(3) Cover frame with available material.

(a) If natural materials are used, arrange them in layers starting at the bottom with each layer overlapping the previous one (figure 4-16).

(b) If porous material is used, that is, parachute, blankets, etc:
   -1. Stretch as tight as possible.
   -2. Use a 40°-60° pitch.
   -3. Use additional layers in heavy rains.

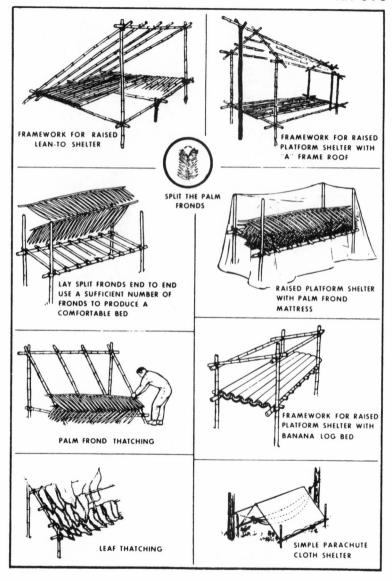

FRAMEWORK FOR RAISED LEAN-TO SHELTER

FRAMEWORK FOR RAISED PLATFORM SHELTER WITH "A" FRAME ROOF

SPLIT THE PALM FRONDS

LAY SPLIT FRONDS END TO END USE A SUFFICIENT NUMBER OF FRONDS TO PRODUCE A COMFORTABLE BED

RAISED PLATFORM SHELTER WITH PALM FROND MATTRESS

PALM FROND THATCHING

FRAMEWORK FOR RAISED PLATFORM SHELTER WITH BANANA LOG BED

LEAF THATCHING

SIMPLE PARACHUTE CLOTH SHELTER

Figure 4-14. Wet Climate Shelters.

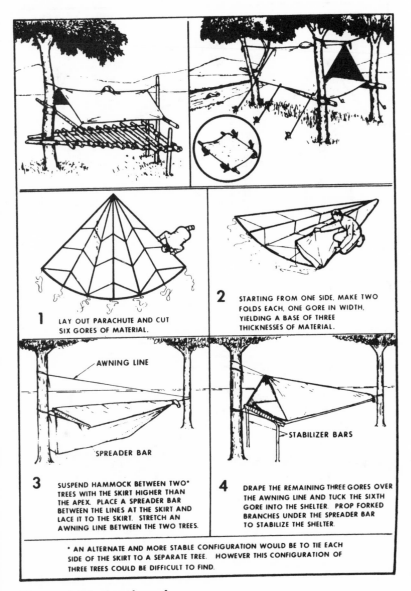

1 LAY OUT PARACHUTE AND CUT SIX GORES OF MATERIAL.

2 STARTING FROM ONE SIDE, MAKE TWO FOLDS EACH, ONE GORE IN WIDTH, YIELDING A BASE OF THREE THICKNESSES OF MATERIAL.

AWNING LINE

SPREADER BAR

3 SUSPEND HAMMOCK BETWEEN TWO* TREES WITH THE SKIRT HIGHER THAN THE APEX. PLACE A SPREADER BAR BETWEEN THE LINES AT THE SKIRT AND LACE IT TO THE SKIRT. STRETCH AN AWNING LINE BETWEEN THE TWO TREES.

STABILIZER BARS

4 DRAPE THE REMAINING THREE GORES OVER THE AWNING LINE AND TUCK THE SIXTH GORE INTO THE SHELTER. PROP FORKED BRANCHES UNDER THE SPREADER BAR TO STABILIZE THE SHELTER.

* AN ALTERNATE AND MORE STABLE CONFIGURATION WOULD BE TO TIE EACH SIDE OF THE SKIRT TO A SEPARATE TREE. HOWEVER THIS CONFIGURATION OF THREE TREES COULD BE DIFFICULT TO FIND.

Figure 4-14. Continued.

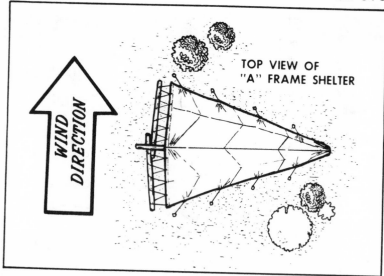

Figure 4-15. Entrance of Shelter.

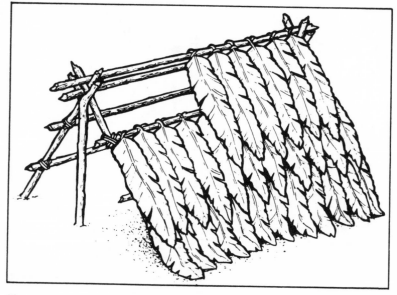

Figure 4-16. Shingle Method.

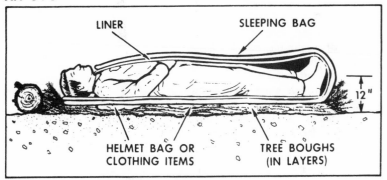

Figure 4-17. Sleeping System.

(4) Construct a bed to protect from the cold, damp ground using (figure 4-17):

(a) Raft turned upside down.

Figure 4-18. Fire Plow.

(b) Boughs, leaves, or dry moss.

(c) Foam rubber from aircraft seats.

(d) Insulation from inside aircraft.

4-3. Starting a Fire:

a. The three essential elements for starting a fire are heat, fuel, and oxygen.

(1) Some heat sources to start fire are:

(a) Matches or lighter.

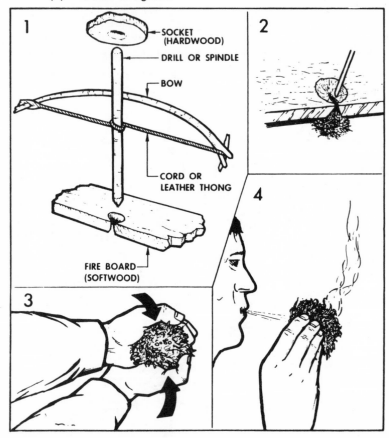

Figure 4-19. Bow and Drill.

Figure 4-20. Bamboo Fire Saw.

(b) Flint and steel (experiment with various rocks and metals until a good spark is produced).

(c) Sparks from batteries.

(d) Concentrated sunlight, using magnifying glass or flashlight reflectors.

(e) Pyrotechnics, such as a flare, etc.

(f) Friction devices (figures 4-18, 4-19, and 4-20).

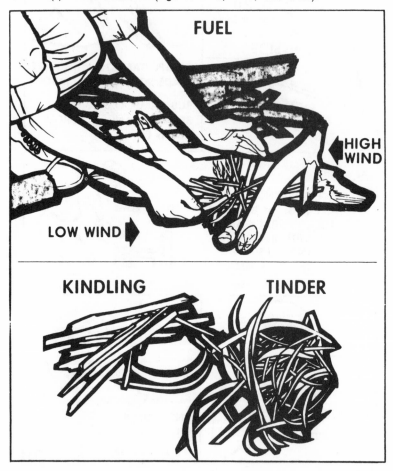

Figure 4-21. Fire Materials.

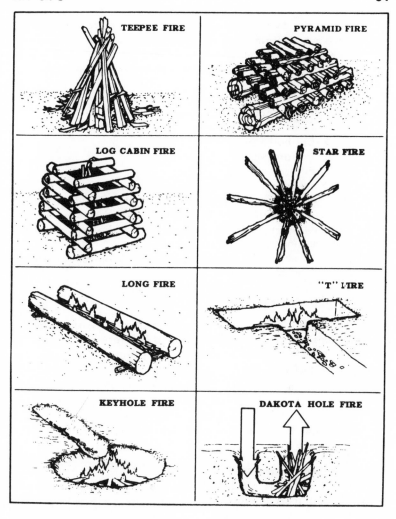

Figure 4-22. Fire Lays.

(2) The element of fuel is divided in three stages—tinder, kindling, and fuel (figure 4-21). Large amounts of each stage should be gathered before igniting the fire.

(a) Tinder must be very finely shaved, or shredded, to provide a low combustion point and fluffed to allow oxygen to flow through. To get tinders to burn hotter and longer, saturate with such things as Vaseline, Chapstick, insect repellant, aircraft fuel, etc. Some tinders are:

      1. Cotton.

      2. Candle (shred the wick, not the wax).

      3. Plastic spoon, fork, or knife.

      4. Foam rubber.

      5. Dry bark.

      6. Dry grasses.

      7. Pitch.

(b) Kindling, the second stage, must be small enough to ignite from the small flame of the tinder. Then gradually build up through larger kindling until arriving at the size of fuel that is to be burned.

(c) Fuel, the third stage, does not have to be kept completely dry. Some fuels include:

      1. Bamboo (chambers must be open to prevent explosion).

      2. Seal blubber.

      3. Dry dui , from plant eating animals.

      4. Peat moss.

b. Fire lays are built to meet specific needs or uses. The following configurations are the most commonly used (figure 4-22):

(1) Teepee fire is used to produce a concentrated heat source used primarily for cooking.

(2) Log cabin or pyramid fires are used to produce large amounts of light and heat, to dry out wet wood, and provide coals for cooking, etc.

(3) Dakota fire hole is a good fire for high winds or evasion situations (figure 4-23).

c. Other heat sources:

(1) Fire reflectors are used to get the most warmth from a fire. Build it against rocks or logs. Don't use porous rocks or river bed rocks—they may explode when heated.

(2) Improvised stoves are good in barren areas (figure 4-24).

d. Banking the fire:

      (1) Build up good bed of coals.

      (2) Cover coals with ashes.

      (3) Cover with dry dirt.

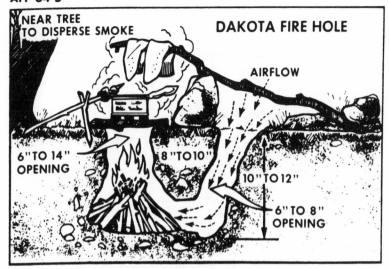

Figure 4-23. Dakota Fire Hole.

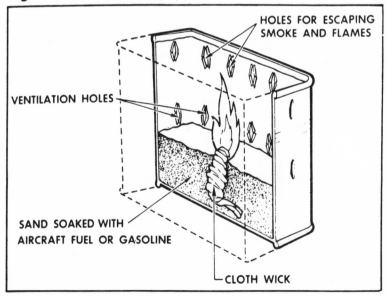

Figure 4-24. Improvised Stove.

(4) To rekindle the fire:
   (a) Remove the dry dirt.
   (b) Lay tinder on hot coals.
   (c) Blow gently until it flames up.

4-4. Other Protective Equipment:

   a. The antiexposure suit works well in water but may also be used on land during windy or rainy periods.

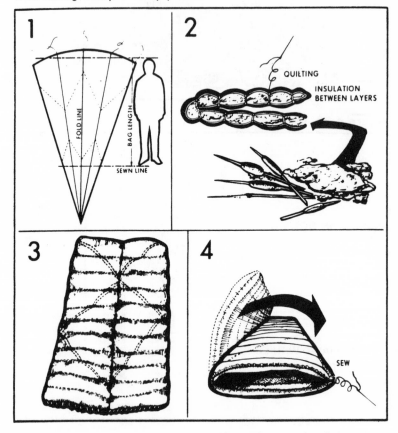

Figure 4-25. Improvised Sleeping Bag.

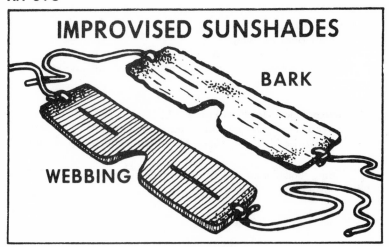

IMPROVISED SUNSHADES

BARK

WEBBING

Figure 4-26. Sun and Snow Goggles.

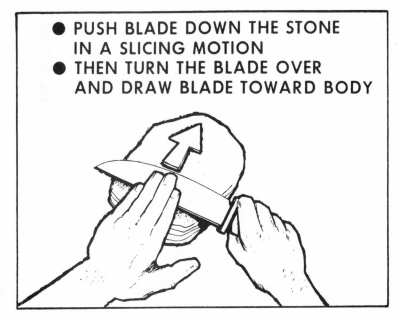

● PUSH BLADE DOWN THE STONE
IN A SLICING MOTION
● THEN TURN THE BLADE OVER
AND DRAW BLADE TOWARD BODY

Figure 4-27. Sharpening Method.

b. Sleeping bag:

   (1) Fluff prior to using.

   (2) Air and dry daily to rid of body moisture.

   (3) May be improvised with parachute material and dry grass, leaves, dry moss, etc. (figure 4-25).

c. Sun and snow goggles (figure 4-26):

   (1) Wear in any bright sun or snow conditions.

   (2) Improvise by cutting small horizontal slits in webbing or bark.

d. Cutting tools should be kept sharp to prevent injury. See figure 4-27 for sharpening method.

Chapter 5

SIGNALING AND RECOVERY

5-1. Signaling Devices and Techniques:

a. Manufactured signals:
(1) Radios and beacons:
(a) Locator beacon will override any voice transmission. Shut it off before using the radio.
(b) Transmit voice as soon as possible after crash or parachute landing, except in hostile areas where transmissions should be accomplished as prebriefed.
(c) The range of the radio is greatly affected by its line of sight characteristics.
1. Move up and out of valleys, drainages, and canyons before transmitting.
2. Use the terrain to mask transmissions from the enemy (figure 5-1).
(d) The battery life of these devices is limited.
1. Keep batteries as warm and dry as possible.
2. Use for short periods of time regularly instead of continuously.
(e) Keep the radio at a right angle to the aircraft to avoid cone of silence.
(2) Strobe light:
(a) Conserve battery life, use when aircraft is spotted.
(b) Use colored shield in hostile areas or when told by rescue.
(3) Pyrotechnic signals:
(a) Become familiar with these devices before they are needed.
(b) They must be kept dry.
(c) Use when an aircraft or ship is sighted or heard. In a hostile area, use as prebriefed or when Rescue requests them.
(4) Sea marker dye:
(a) Use during daylight.
(b) Do not waste in rough water.
(c) Conserve unused dye by rewrapping.
(d) May be used to color snow.
(e) Effective in streams and rivers.

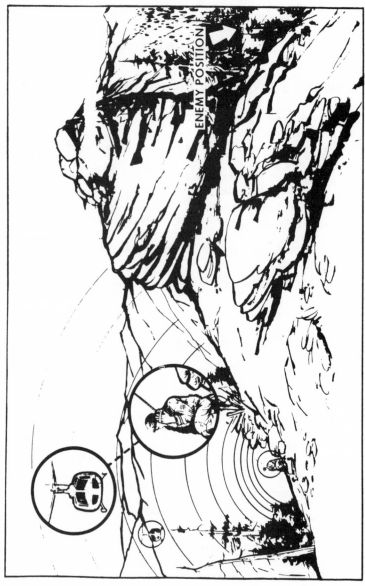

Figure 5-1. Transmission Location.

(5) Audio signals are used to attract ground and water search parties.

    (a) Voice.

    (b) Whistle.

    (c) Weapon fire.

    (d) Striking hollow trees and logs.

(6) Signal paulin and space blankets:

    (a) Different color on each side.

    (b) Fold in various patterns for different messages.

(7) Signal mirror:

    (a) Instructions for use are printed on the back (figure 5-2).

    (b) Sweep the horizon constantly whether aircraft is in sight or not.

    (c) In hostile areas, use only on authenticated targets and cover when not in use.

  b. Improvised signals:

    (1) Signal mirror can be made from any shiny metal or glass.

    (2) Fire and smoke signals:

      (a) Use campfire for signal.

        1. Conserves fuel and energy.

        2. Maintain supply of rapid burning materials to throw on quickly.

      (b) During the day use smoke that contrasts with surrounding area.

        1. To produce dark smoke use:

          a. Oil-soaked rags.

          b. Rubber.

          c. Plastic.

          d. Electrical insulation.

        2. For white smoke use:

          a. Green leaves.

          b. Moss.

          c. Ferns.

          d. Water sprinkled on fire.

        3. A smoke generator could be constructed (figure 5-3).

      (c) Burn bright fires at night.

    (3) Pattern signals (figure 5-4).

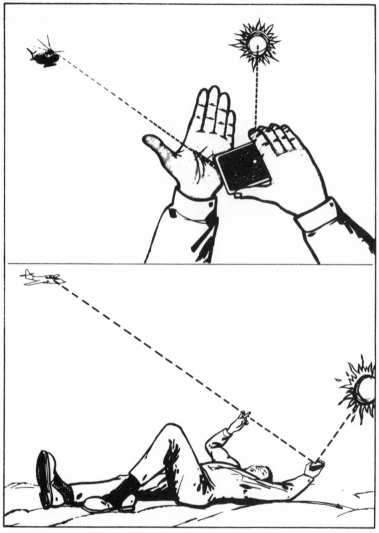

Figure 5-2. Sighting Techniques.

    (a) Location of signal:
        1. High and clear as possible.
        2. In hostile areas, the site should be seen only from the air.

LOTS OF DEAD-DRY TWIGS OR KINDLING FOR QUICK STARTING FAST BURNING FIRE

EVERGREEN BOUGHS

SMALL OPENING FOR LIGHTING FIRE

Figure 5-3. Smoke Generator.

(b) Size and ratio (figure 5-5).

(c) Maintain straight lines and sharp corners (figure 5-6).

(d) Contrast with surrounding area, using:

1. Colored parachute material. (Do not use orange material against green background.)

No.	Message	Code Symbol
1	Require Assistance	**V**
2	Require Medical Assistance	**X**
3	No or Negative	**N**
4	Yes or Affirmative	**Y**
5	Proceeding In This Direction	**↑**

Figure 5-4. Signal Meanings.

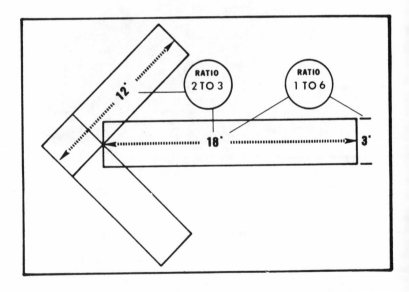

Figure 5-5. Size and Ratio.

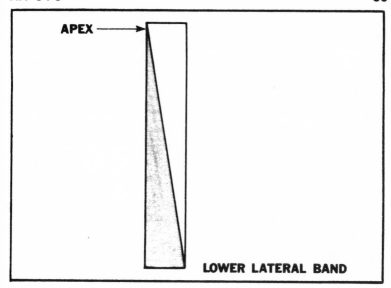

Figure 5-6. Parachute Material.

       2. Shadows produced by:

            a. Piling rocks, brush, or snow. Remember the movement of the sun.

            b. Scraping or tramping out trenches in weeds, dirt, sand, or snow.

            c. Elevating parachute material.

     (e) In hostile areas, signal should be constructed so that it can be removed quickly and as briefed in the premission briefing.

    (4) Look and listen for acknowledgement from Rescue (figure 5-7).

5-2. Recovery Procedures:

  a. Survivors' responsibilities:

    (1) Attempt to make radio contact with Rescue.

    (2) Build and maintain ground signals.

    (3) Follow instructions of rescue personnel.

    (4) Additional responsibilities in hostile areas:

      (a) Follow prebriefed radio procedures.

      (b) Authenticate self and rescue aircraft.

      (c) Keep Rescue informed of enemy activities.

MESSAGE RECEIVED AND UNDERSTOOD
AIRCRAFT WILL INDICATE THAT GROUND SIGNALS HAVE BEEN SEEN AND UNDERSTOOD BY—

DAY OR MOONLIGHT: ROCKING FROM SIDE TO SIDE

NIGHT: MAKING GREEN FLASHES WITH SIGNAL LAMP

MESSAGE RECEIVED BUT NOT UNDERSTOOD
AIRCRAFT WILL INDICATE THAT GROUND SIGNALS HAVE BEEN SEEN BUT NOT UNDERSTOOD BY—

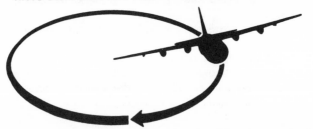

DAY OR MOONLIGHT: MAKING A COMPLETE RIGHT HAND CIRCLE

NIGHT: MAKING RED FLASHES WITH SIGNAL LAMP

Figure 5-7. Standard Aircraft Acknowledgements.

b. Recovery site:

(1) Pick high terrain in immediate area. (In combat area, consider terrain masking for SAR aircraft.)

(2) Check for any obstacles.

(3) Additional considerations for hostile areas:

(a) Observe site for 24 hours for signs of human activity.

(b) Locate several good hiding places around the area.

(c) Plan several escape routes to avoid being trapped by the enemy.

c. Recovery procedures:

(1) Secure anything that could be caught up in helicopter rotors or boat propellers, that is, parachute canopy, lanyards, sea anchor, etc.

(2) Be prepared for any type of rescue vehicle and follow instructions given.

(a) Boats and ships:

1. Do not swim or paddle toward or away from ship or boat.

2. Survivor normally will not be required to assist.

(b) Helicopter landing:

1. Stay clear until aircraft is on the ground. Stay hidden in hostile areas.

2. Wait until crew member comes out to assist or signal to come aboard, although, in hostile areas this may not always be possible.

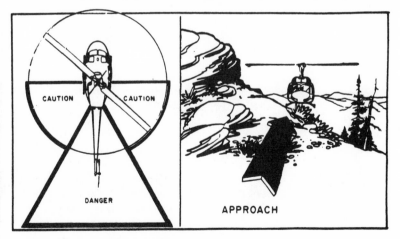

Figure 5-8. Helicopter Danger Zones.

3. Approach aircraft from 9 to 3 o'clock position depending on door location, instructions, etc. (figure 5-8); double-rotor helicopters from the rear.

(c) Helicopters with pickup devices:

1. Stand clear until device has grounded out.

2. Sit or kneel for stability while donning the device.

3. Put on safety straps first.

    a. Ensure that the strap goes under armpits.

    b. Ensure the cable is in front.

4. Keep hands clear of cable and connectors.

5. Use the radio, a thumbs up, or a vigorous shake of the cable to signal the hoist operator for pickup.

6. Do not assist the crew while being hoisted and follow instructions.

7. Army helicopters may drop a device to be donned while they make another pass and drop a rope to be hooked into the device. If you don't know how to use the device as designed, make a "fixed loop" out of the device. In hostile areas, expect to be flown away without being lifted (may not have hoist capability) into the helicopter immediately.

Chapter 6

TRAVEL TECHNIQUES

6-1. The Decision to Stay or Travel:

a. Stay with the aircraft, if possible.

b. Leave only when:

(1) Certain of present location, have a known destination, and the ability to get there.

(2) Water, food, shelter, and (or) help can be reached.

(3) Convinced that rescue is not coming.

c. If the decision is to travel, the following must also be considered:

(1) Which direction to travel and why.

(2) What plan is to be followed.

(3) What equipment should be taken.

(4) How to mark a trail (figure 6-1).

d. Leave information at the departure point which states:

(1) Departure time.

(2) Destination.

(3) Route of travel.

(4) Personal condition.

(5) Available supplies.

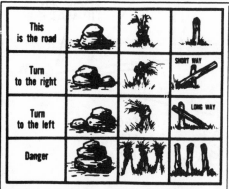

Figure 6-1. Trail Markings.

6-2. Navigation and Position Determination:

a. Determine general location:

    (1) A working knowledge of operational area.

       (a) Natural geographic checkpoints.

       (b) Manmade checkpoints.

    (2) Use the "Rate × Time = Distance" formula:

       (a) Rate of speed of aircraft.

       (b) Total length of flight.

       (c) Direction of flight.

       (d) Length of time in air before crash or emergency.

    (3) Determine cardinal direction (north, south, east, or west).

       (a) Stick and shadow may be used to determine (figure 6-2):

          1. Cardinal direction.

          2. Local apparent noon.

       (b) Sunrise in the east, sunset in the west.

    (4) A wristwatch may be used to determine cardinal direction (figure 6-3).

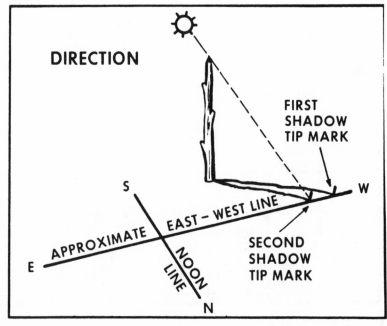

Figure 6-2. Stick and Shadow.

(5) Celestial aids (figure 6-4).

    (a) Use Polaris to locate true north-south line.

    (b) Use Southern Cross to locate true north-south line.

(6) Orient map to true north (figure 6-5):

    (a) Use previous knowledge of operational area.

    (b) Use information provided in the legend.

    (c) Prominent landmarks.

    (d) If compass not available, use cardinal direction attained by:

        1. Stick and shadow (figure 6-2).

        2. Celestial aids (figure 6-4).

    (e) Use compass (figure 6-5).

    (f) Visualize map to try to determine position (figure 6-6).

b. Determine specific location:

    (1) Triangulating with a compass (figure 6-7):

        (a) Try to use three or more azimuths.

        (b) Each time compass is put on the map, check map orientation.

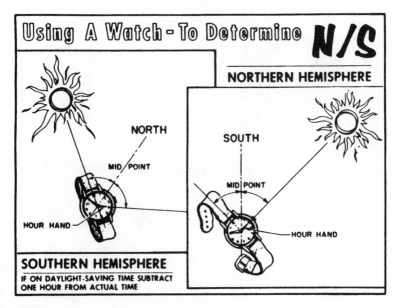

Figure 6-3. Direction Using a Watch.

(2) Triangulating without a compass (figure 6-8).

(3) If you don't have a map (nontactical), improvise one and keep track of where you have been.

c. Use the compass for night navigation (figure 6-9).

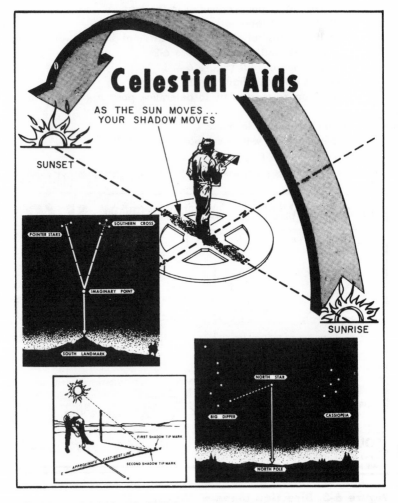

Figure 6-4. Celestial Aids.

d. Use of map:
　　(1) Do not write on evasion map.
　　(2) Do not soil map by touching destination on map.
　　(3) Do not fold map in a manner which provides travel information.

e. Route selection techniques:
　　(1) Circumnavigation:
　　　　(a) Find prominent landmark on the opposite side of obstacle that is on your route of travel (figure 6-10).
　　　　(b) Contour around obstacle to landmark.
　　　　(c) Resume your route of travel.
　　(2) Dogleg:
　　　　(a) When you come to an obstacle, take a 45° turn off of your heading (figure 6-11).
　　　　(b) Walk, keeping track of paces, or amount of time until you're past the obstacle.

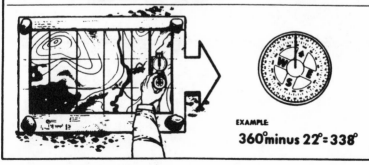

USING THE MAP & COMPASS TOGETHER
ORIENTING A MAP
1. **PLACE MAP ON FIRM LEVEL SURFACE.**
2. **LINE UP COMPASS ON MAP TO A TRUE NORTH-SOUTH LINE.**
3. **TURN MAP UNTIL STATIONARY INDEX LINE IS ALIGNED WITH THE MAGNETIC VARIATION INDICATED.**

EXAMPLE:
360° minus 22° = 338°

Figure 6-5. Map Orientation.

(c) Turn 90° back toward your original heading and walk back the same number of paces or amount of time.

(d) Resume original headings.

(3) Straight line heading. Maintain a constant heading until destination is reached.

(a) 1200 paces per mile (average).

(b) 1800 paces per mile in rough terrain (average).

(c) Pace is every time the same foot touches ground.

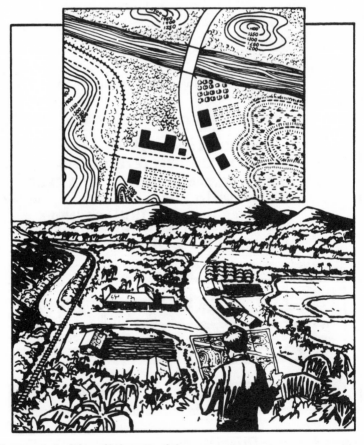

Figure 6-6. Visualizing Position.

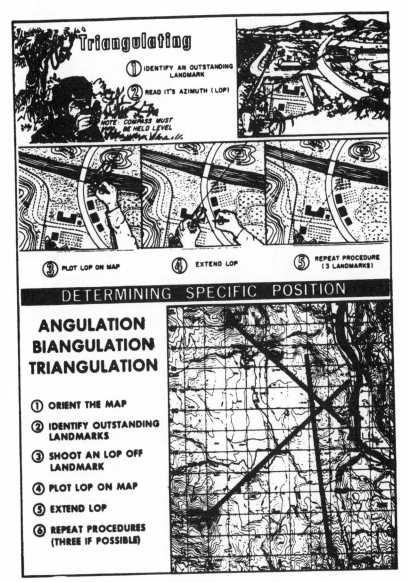

Figure 6-7. Triangulation.

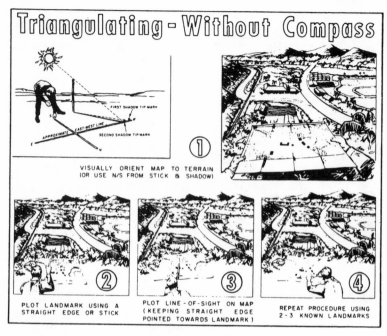

Figure 6-8. Triangulating Without a Compass.

(d) Deliberate offset:
1. Compensates for possible error.
2. User knows whether to go right or left to reach objective.

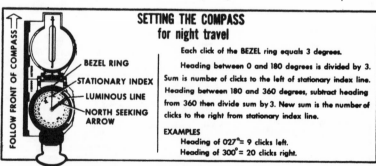

Figure 6-9. Night Navigation.

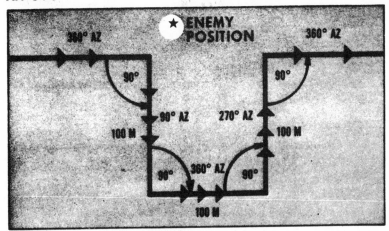

Figure 6-10. Circumnavigation.

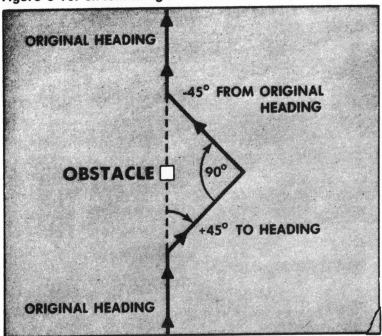

Figure 6-11. Dogleg.

(4) Point-to-point:

    (a) Same as straight line.

    (b) Pick out landmarks which are on the heading and walk the trail of least resistance to point.

    (c) After making that point, establish another point and continue.

6-3. Travel:

a. Maintain a realistic pace.

b. Rest stops should be taken when needed.

c. Avoid overdressing and overheating.

d. Nutrition and water must be considered.

e. Take special care of feet.

f. Pack equipment to preclude loss or damage, pack balance, and personal safety.

6-4. Travel Hints:

a. Pick the easiest and safest route (except for evasion).

b. Go around obstacles instead of over or through them.

c. Traverse up a slope.

d. Go around the edges of gullies or canyons (except during evasion).

e. Don't penetrate swamps or mud flats if you can go around.

6-5. River Travel (figure 6-12):

a. Saves energy.

b. Travel faster.

c. In shallow water, use a pole to move the raft.

d. In deeper water, use an oar.

e. Travel on rivers only during daylight.

f. Stay near inside edge of river bends.

g. Keep near shore.

h. Watch for *dangers:*

    (1) Snags.

    (2) Sweepers—overhanging limbs and trees.

    (3) Rapids.

    (4) Waterfalls.

i. Do not attempt to shoot the rapids.

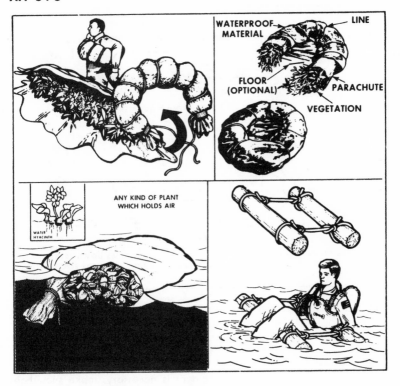

Figure 6-12. Flotation Systems.

    j. When crossing a river or stream, use:
      (1) A raft.
      (2) Fording techniques (figure 6-13).

6-6. Ice and Snow Areas:

    a. Travel should be limited to:
      (1) Movement away from an unsafe area.
      (2) Movement to enhance personal protection.

    b. Don't travel in:
      (1) Blizzards.
      (2) Bitter cold winds.

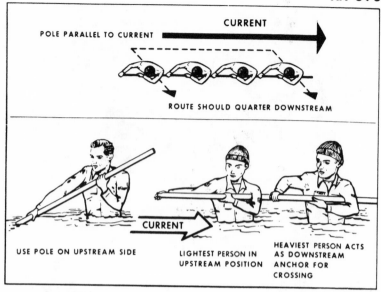

CURRENT

POLE PARALLEL TO CURRENT

ROUTE SHOULD QUARTER DOWNSTREAM

CURRENT

USE POLE ON UPSTREAM SIDE

LIGHTEST PERSON IN UPSTREAM POSITION

HEAVIEST PERSON ACTS AS DOWNSTREAM ANCHOR FOR CROSSING

Figure 6-13. Stream Crossing.

    (3) Poor visibility.

  c. Obstacles to winter travel:

    (1) Deep soft snow; if movement is necessary, make snowshoes (figure 6-14).

    (2) Dangerous river ice:

      (a) Weak ice should be expected where:

        1. Rivers are straight.

        2. Objects protrude through ice.

        3. Snow banks extend over the ice.

        4. Two rivers or streams come together.

      (b) Air pockets where a frozen river has suddenly lost volume.

    (3) Glacier travel is extremely hazardous and should be avoided.

  d. Obstacles to summer travel:

    (1) Dense brush:

      (a) Travel on trails whenever possible (nontactical).

      (b) Travel in forested areas if possible.

      (c) Avoid creek bottoms and ravine floors.

    (2) Rough terrain (figure 6-15).

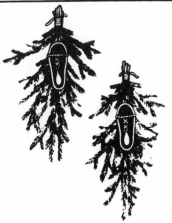

CANADIAN EMERGENCY SNOWSHOES

1. Select 6 poles 6 feet long (individual's height), ¾ inch (thumb size) at the base, ¼ inch (little finger size) at the tip. Cut 6 sticks approximately 10 inches long and ¾ inches wide and tie them in the following manner:

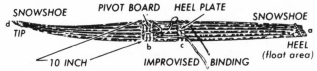

SNOWSHOE TIP — PIVOT BOARD — HEEL PLATE — SNOWSHOE — HEEL (float area) — 10 INCH — IMPROVISED BINDING

   a. Lash one stick to the snowshoe float area (cut off excess).

   b. Lash three sticks forward of the center of the shoe to form the pivot board. This position of the pivot board allows the float to remain on the snow and causes the tip to rise when walking.

   c. Lash two sticks where your heel strikes the snowshoe to form the heel plate.

   d. Tie the snowshoe tips together.

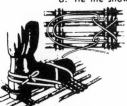

2. The snowshoe binding must be secured to the snowshoe so that the survivor's foot can pivot when walking.

Binding — make as shown from continuous length of split harness webbing or from suspension lines (braided lines preferred).

Figure 6-14. Improvised Snowshoes.

Figure 6-15. Rough Terrain Foot Placement.

    (3) Soft ground:
        (a) Step on rocks, twigs, and vegetation.
        (b) Step lightly, checking for firm ground.
        (c) Improvised snowshoes can be used.
    (4) Swamps, lakes, and unfordable rivers:
        (a) Swamps and lakes may have to be circumnavigated.
        (b) Travel downstream to find people and slower water.
        (c) Travel upstream to find narrower and shallower water.

  e. Head for:
    (1) A coast.
    (2) A major river.
    (3) A known point of habitation.

  f. Make camp early.

6-7. Dry Climates:

a. Don't travel unless certain of reaching the destination using the water supply available.

b. When the days are hot, travel during dawn, dusk, or evening.

c. Head for:
   (1) A coast.
   (2) A known route of travel.
   (3) A water source.
   (4) An inhabited area.

d. Follow the easiest trail possible (nontactical). Avoid:
   (1) Soft sand.
   (2) Rough terrain.

e. If a sandstorm occurs:
   (1) Mark your direction of travel.
   (2) Sit or lie down.
   (3) Try to get to the lee side of any natural shelter.
   (4) Cover the mouth and nose with a piece of cloth.
   (5) Protect the eyes.
   (6) Stay put until the storm blows over.

f. In sand dune areas:
   (1) Follow hard floor valleys between the dunes.
   (2) Travel on the windward side of dune ridges.

6-8. Hot, Wet Climates:

a. Travel only when it is light.

b. Avoid obstacles such as thickets and swamps.

c. Part the vegetation to pass through.

d. Don't climb over logs if you can go around them.

e. Find a trail and follow it.
   (1) Trails can be found:
      (a) Where two streams meet.
      (b) Where a low pass goes over a range of hills.
      (c) At rapids.
   (2) While traveling trails:
      (a) Don't follow a trail which is obviously closed as it may lead to an animal trap.
      (b) Watch for disturbed areas on game trails—they may indicate a pitfall or trap.
      (c) Don't sleep on a game trail.

f. Go downhill until you find a stream, then follow the stream. The best chance of finding people is along trails, streams, and along coastlines.

6-9. Open Seas:

a. Use of currents:

(1) Deploy sea anchor (figure 6-16). Sea anchor may be adjusted to make maximum use of existing currents.

(2) Sit low in the raft.

(3) Let some air out of the raft so it will ride lower in the water.

b. Use of winds:

(1) Pull in sea anchor.

(2) Inflate raft so it rides higher.

(3) Sit up in raft so body catches the wind.

(4) Construct a sail (figure 6-17).

c. Making landfall:

(1) Indication of land:

(a) Fixed cumulus clouds in a clear sky or in a cloudy sky where all other clouds are moving.

(b) In the tropics, a greenish tint in the sky.

(c) In the arctic, lighter colored reflections on clouds (open water causes darkish grey reflections).

(d) Lighter colored water indicates shallow water.

(e) Land may be detected by odors and sounds.

1. Odors from swamps and smoke.

2. Roar of surf and cries from birds coming from one direction.

(f) Direction from which sea birds fly at dawn and to which they fly at dark.

(2) Swimming ashore:

(a) Some type of flotation aid should be used.

(b) Wear footgear and at least one layer of clothing.

(c) The side or breast stroke will help conserve strength.

(d) If the surf is moderate:

1. Swim forward on the back of a wave.

2. Make a shallow dive just before the wave breaks to end the ride.

(e) If there is high surf:

1. Swim shoreward in the trough between waves.

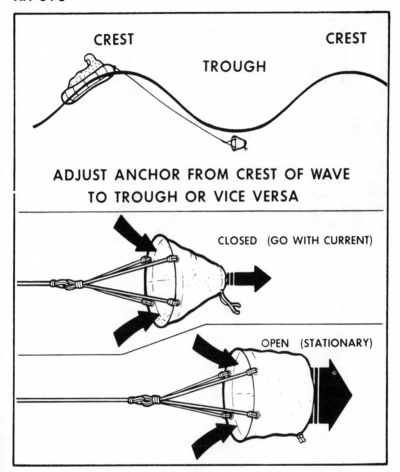

CREST

TROUGH

CREST

**ADJUST ANCHOR FROM CREST OF WAVE
TO TROUGH OR VICE VERSA**

CLOSED (GO WITH CURRENT)

OPEN (STATIONARY)

Figure 6-16. Deployment of Sea Anchor.

      2. When the seaward wave approaches, face it and submerge.

      3. After it passes, work shoreward in the next trough.

  (f) If caught in the undertow of a large wave:

    1. Push off from the bottom or swim to the surface.

    2. Lie as close to the surface as possible.

    3. Swim shoreward.

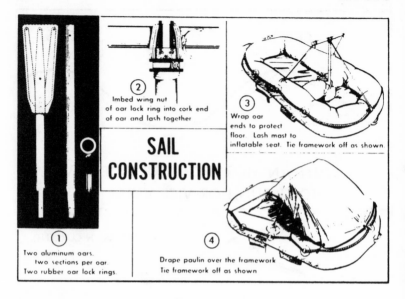

Figure 6-17. Sail Construction.

(g) Selecting a landing point:

1. Avoid places where waves explode upon rocks.

2. If you must land on rocky shores, select a place where waves rush up onto the rocks.

(h) After selecting a landing site:

1. Face shoreward.

2. Assume a sitting position with feet two or three feet lower than the head to absorb the shock of hitting submerged objects.

(3) Rafting ashore:

(a) Select landing point carefully.

(b) Use caution while landing when the sun is low and straight in front of you causing poor visibility.

(c) Land on the lee (downwind) side of an island or point of land.

(d) Head for gaps in the surf line.

(e) When going through surf:

1. Take down mast.

2. Don clothing and shoes to avoid injuries.

3. Adjust and fasten life preserver.

4. Stow equipment.

5. Use paddles to maintain control.

6. Ensure sea anchor is deployed for stability.

CAUTION: The sea anchor should *not* be deployed when traveling through coral.

(f) Sea ice landings should be made on large stable ice floes.

(g) Icebergs, small floes, and disintegrating floes could cause serious problems.

1. Ice can cut a raft.

2. Use paddles to keep away from sharp edges.

3. Store raft away from the ice edge.

4. Keep raft inflated and ready for use.

5. Weight down or secure the raft so the wind won't blow it away.

Chapter 7

SUSTENANCE

7-1. Water Procurement:

a. Water requirements:

(1) Adults require a minimum of 2 to 3 quarts of water daily.

(a) Temperature extremes.

    1. In hot climates:

        a. Essential activities should be conducted at night or during the cooler part of the day.

        b. Clothing should be worn to reduce sweating.

        c. Wear light colored clothing.

    2. In ice and snow areas:

        a. Avoid overdressing.

        b. Wear a scarf over the nose and mouth.

(b) Activity. Conserve water by limiting physical activity.

(c) Altitude. Lack of oxygen requires more water.

(d) Injury or illness. Creates a need for water.

(2) Drink as much water as possible to maintain body fluid level.

b. Water sources (general):

(1) Surface water:

(a) Streams.

(b) Lakes.

(c) Springs.

(2) Precipitation (figures 7-1 and 7-2):

(a) Rain

(b) Snow.

(c) Dew.

(d) Sleet.

(3) Subsurface:

(a) Wells.

(b) Cisterns.

c. Indicators of possible water sources:

(1) Abundance of vegetation.

(2) Drainages and low lying areas.

(3) Large clumps of lush grass.

(4) The "V" of intersecting game trails often point toward water.

(5) The presence of swarming insects indicates water is near.

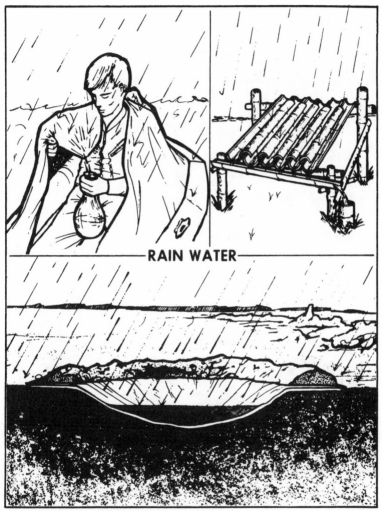

Figure 7-1. Precipitation Catches.

(6) Bird flight in the early morning or late afternoon might indicate the direction to water.

d. When no surface water is available, ground water could possibly be obtained by looking in areas such as depicted in figure 7-3.

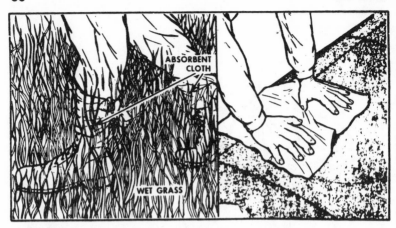

Figure 7-2. Moisture Collectors.

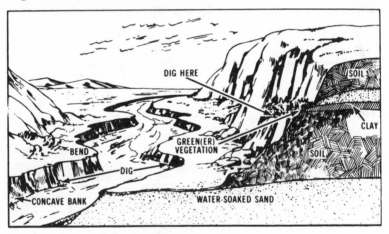

Figure 7-3. Water Locations.

    e. Snow and ice areas:
        (1) Do not eat ice or snow.
            (a) Lowers body temperature.
            (b) Induces dehydration.
            (c) Causes minor cold injury to lips and mouth.
        (2) Snow machine (figure 7-4).

Figure 7-4. Snow Machine.

    (3) Melt ice or snow with body heat.
      (a) Use waterproof container.
      (b) Place between layers of clothing.
      (c) *Do not* place next to the skin.
    (4) Sea ice (use old sea ice):

OLD SEA ICE	NEW SEA ICE
Bluish or blackish	Milky or grey
Shatters easily	Doesn't break easily
Rounded corners	Sharp edges
Tastes relatively salt-free	Tastes extremely salty

  f. Open seas:
    (1) Precipitation:
      (a) Drink as much as possible.

    (b) Catch rain in spray shields and life raft covers.

(2) Use issued sources.

(3) Old sea ice or iceberg.

(4) *Do not* drink:

    (a) Urine.

    (b) Fish juices.

    (c) Blood.

    (d) Sea water.

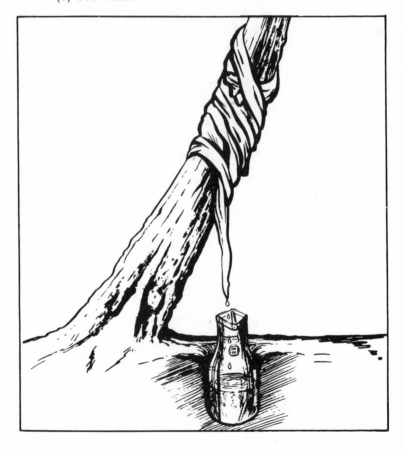

Figure 7-5. Leaning Tree.

g. Water sources (tropical areas):

(1) All open sources previously mentioned.

(2) Vegetation:

(a) Plants that have hollow portions which can collect moisture.

(b) Leaning tree. Cloth absorbs rain running down tree and drips into container (figure 7-5).

(c) Banana plants (figure 7-6).

(d) Water trees (figure 7-7):

1. Tap before dark. Let sap stop running and harden during the daytime.

2. Produce most water at night.

3. For evasion situations, bore into the roots and collect water.

(e) Vines:

1. Cut bark - milky sap—do not use.

2. If juice is clear and waterlike, cut as large a piece of vine as possible, cutting the top first.

3. Pour into hand to check smell, color, and taste to determine if drinkable.

4. Do not touch vine to lips.

THE BANANA OR PLANTAIN TRUNK CAN BE AN IDEAL SOURCE OF WATER. CUT THROUGH THE TRUNK ABOUT 3 INCHES ABOVE GROUND. HOLLOW-OUT A BOWL-LIKE RESERVOIR. WATER WILL FLOW INTO THE BOWL FROM THE ROOTS. ALLOW THE BOWL TO FILL THEN SCOOP OUT WATER UNTIL PALATABLE. THE SAME TRUNK CAN BE USED FOR UP TO 4 DAYS. COVER WHEN NOT IN USE.

CUT OUT BOWL

CUT HERE

WATER WILL FILL BOWL FROM ROOTS

Figure 7-6. Banana Plant.

Figure 7-7. Water Trees.

       5. When water flow stops, cut off 6 inches of opposite end, water will flow again.

      (f) Bamboo:

        1. Old bamboo:

          a. Shake and listen for water.

          b. Bore hole at bottom of section to obtain the water.

          c. Cut out entire section to carry with you.

          d. Filter and purify.

        2. Green bamboo (figure 7-8 and a, b, and c above).

      (g) Along the coast, water may be obtained by:

        1. Digging a beach well (figure 7-9).

       2. Liquid contained in ripe coconuts may cause diarrhea and increase dehydration; use in small quantities.

Figure 7-8. Green Bamboo.

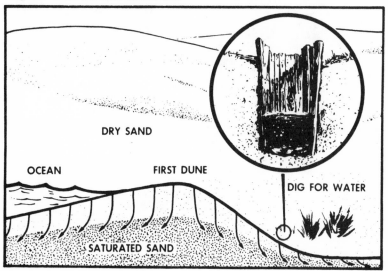

DRY SAND

OCEAN

FIRST DUNE

DIG FOR WATER

SATURATED SAND

Figure 7-9. Beach Well.

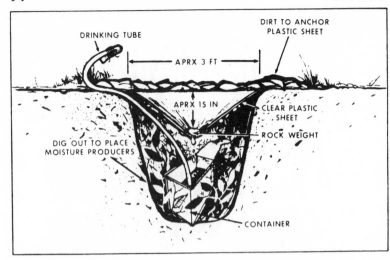

Figure 7-10. Solar Still.

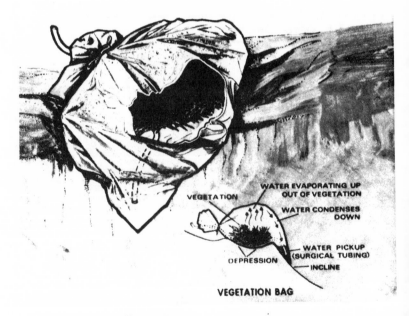

Figure 7-11. Foliage Bag.

Figure 7-12. Transpiration Bag.

(3) Dry areas:
(a) Solar still (figure 7-10).

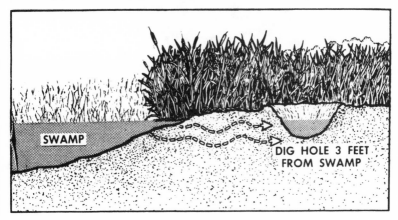

Figure 7-13. Seepage Basin.

(b) Foliage bag (figure 7-11).

(c) Transpiration bag (figure 7-12):

　1. Water bag must be clear.

　2. Water will taste like the plant smells.

h. Water Preparation:

　(1) Filtration:

　　(a) Seepage basin (figure 7-13).

　　(b) Construct a filter (figure 7-14).

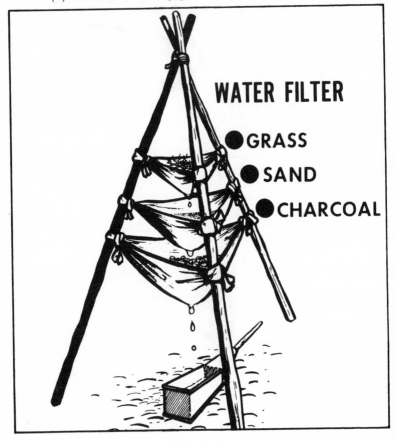

Figure 7-14. Filtration Method.

(2) Purification:

(a) Water produced by live plants requires no further treatment.

(b) All other water should be purified:

1. Boil for at least 10 minutes.

2. To improve taste, aerate by pouring from one container to another.

3. Water purification tablets. Follow instructions.

(c) If water cannot be purified, as in an evasion situation, obtain water from a source which is clear, cold, clean, and fast running (if possible).

(3) Storage. Use a clean container which can be sealed or covered to prevent contamination.

(a) Water bag.

(b) Prophylactic.

(c) Section of bamboo.

(d) LPU bladder.

(e) Hood from antiexposure suit.

7-2. Food Procurement:

a. Sources of animal life:

(1) Fur bearing animals.

(2) Birds.

(3) Fish and other marine life.

(4) Insects.

(5) Reptiles and amphibians.

b. Locating:

(1) Fur bearing animals:

(a) Game trails leading to watering, feeding, and bedding areas.

(b) Look for fresh droppings or tracks.

(2) Birds:

(a) Observe the direction of flight in the early morning and late afternoon.

1. They may lead to their feeding, watering, and roosting areas.

2. Nesting areas may be discovered.

(b) The noise of birds may indicate nesting areas.

(3) Fish and other marine life:

(a) Streams and rivers (figure 7-15).

Figure 7-15. Fishing Locations.

    (b) Lakes, ponds, and oceans.
    (c) Along shores.
  (4) Reptiles and amphibians can be located almost anywhere in the world.
  (5) Insects may also be found worldwide:
    (a) In dead logs and stumps.
    (b) Ant and termite mounds.
    (c) On ponds, lakes, and slow moving streams.
  (6) Hairy insects should be avoided as the hairs could cause irritation or infection.
  (7) Poisonous insects should be avoided, for example:
    (a) Centipedes.
    (b) Scorpions.
    (c) Poisonous spiders.
  (8) Insects which commonly carry diseases should be avoided, for example:
    (a) Flies.

      (b) Mosquitoes.

      (c) Ticks.

   c. Procurement techniques:

     (1) Snares:

      (a) Work while unattended.

      (b) Location of snares:

         1. Frequently used game trails leading to watering, feeding, and bedding areas.

         2. Look for fresh droppings or tracks.

         3. At the mouth of dens (figure 7-16).

      (c) Construction of simple loop snare:

         1. Materials should be those which will not break under the strain of holding an animal.

         2. If wire is being used, a figure-eight (locking loop) should be used (figure 7-17).

Figure 7-16. Snare Placement.

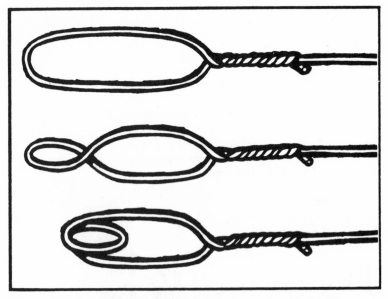

Figure 7-17. Locking Loop.

3. Once tightened around the animal, the wire is locked into place by the figure-eight. This prevents it from opening again and allowing the animal to escape.

4. Simple loop snares can also be used to construct a squirrel pole (figure 7-18).

5. Make noose opening slightly larger than the animal's head, three-finger width for squirrels and fist-sized for rabbits.

(d) Placement of snares:

1. Avoid disturbing the area.

2. Use funneling (natural or improvised) (figure 7-19).

3. Set as many snares as possible.

4. Mark area for ease of relocation.

(2) A noose stick may be easier and safer to use than the hands (figure 7-20).

(3) Twist stick:

(a) Insert forked stick into a den until something soft is met.

(b) Twist the stick, binding the animal's hide in the fork.

(c) Remove the animal from the den.

(d) Be ready to kill the animal as it may be dangerous.

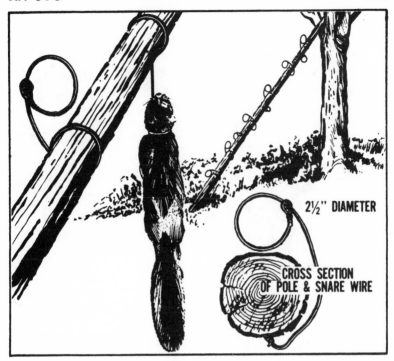

2½" DIAMETER

CROSS SECTION OF POLE & SNARE WIRE

Figure 7-18. Squirrel Pole.

    (4) Killing and wounding devices:
       (a) Club or rock.
       (b) Spear.
       (c) Bow and arrow.
       (d) Sling shot (figure 7-21).
    (5) Pole, line, and hook (figure 7-22).
    (6) Net.
    (7) Trap.
    (8) Foraging along water's edge.
  d. Precautions to observe while obtaining aquatic foods:
    (1) Wear shoes to protect the feet while wading in the water.
    (2) Avoid reaching into dark holes.
    (3) Don't secure fishing lines to yourself or the raft.
    (4) Kill fish before bringing them into the raft.

Figure 7-19. Funneling.

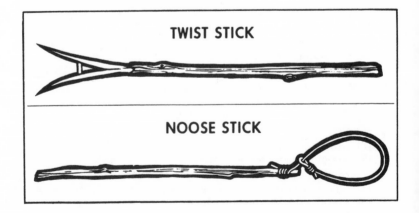

Figure 7-20. Procurement Devices.

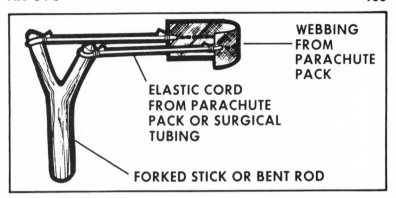

Figure 7-21. Improvised Sling Shot.

Figure 7-22. Procurement Methods.

(5) Don't eat fish with (figure 7-23):

    (a) Unpleasant odor.

    (b) Pale, slimy gills.

    (c) Sunken eyes.

    (d) Flabby skin.

    (e) Flesh which remains dented when pressed.

(6) Don't eat fish eggs or liver (entrails).

(7) Avoid all crustaceans above the high tide mark.

(8) Avoid all aquatic life during a red tide.

(9) Avoid cone-shaped shells.

  e. Plant Foods:

    (1) General rules:

(a) Mushrooms and fungi should not be selected as a food possibility.

(b) Avoid plants with umbrella-shaped flower clusters (figure 7-24).

(c) All beans and peas should be avoided.

(d) As a general rule, all bulbs should be avoided.

(e) White and yellow berries should be avoided as they are almost always poisonous.

(f) Approximately one-half of all red berries are poisonous.

(g) Blue and black berries are generally safe for consumption.

(h) Aggregated berries are (usually) safe for consumption (for example, thimbleberry, raspberry, blackberry, salmonberry).

(i) Single fruits on a stem are generally considered safe to eat.

(j) Plants with shiny leaves should be considered poisonous.

(k) A milky sap indicates a possible poisonous plant.

(l) Plants which are irritants to the skin should not be eaten (for example, poison ivy).

(m) Select a plant which grows in sufficient quantity in the local area.

(n) Apply the edibility test to only one plant at a time. If ill effects occur, it will be obvious which plant caused the problem.

    (2) Edibility test:

(a) Touch the plant's sap or juice to the inner forearm or tip of the tongue (a small taste of a poisonous plant will not do serious harm).

(b) If no ill effects are encountered, such as a rash or bitter taste, numbing sensation, etc., then proceed with the rest of the steps.

(c) Boil the plant or plant part in two changes of water. The toxic properties of many plants are water soluble or are destroyed by heat.

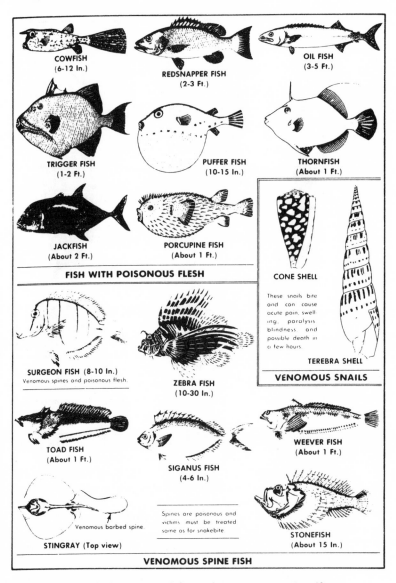

FISH WITH POISONOUS FLESH

COWFISH
(6-12 In.)

REDSNAPPER FISH
(2-3 Ft.)

OIL FISH
(3-5 Ft.)

TRIGGER FISH
(1-2 Ft.)

PUFFER FISH
(10-15 In.)

THORNFISH
(About 1 Ft.)

JACKFISH
(About 2 Ft.)

PORCUPINE FISH
(About 1 Ft.)

CONE SHELL

These snails bite and can cause acute pain, swelling, paralysis blindness and possible death in a few hours.

TEREBRA SHELL

VENOMOUS SNAILS

SURGEON FISH (8-10 In.)
Venomous spines and poisonous flesh.

ZEBRA FISH
(10-30 In.)

TOAD FISH
(About 1 Ft.)

SIGANUS FISH
(4-6 In.)

WEEVER FISH
(About 1 Ft.)

Venomous barbed spine.

STINGRAY (Top view)

Spines are poisonous and victims must be treated same as for snakebite

STONEFISH
(About 15 In.)

VENOMOUS SPINE FISH

Figure 7-23. Poisonous Fish and Venomous Snails.

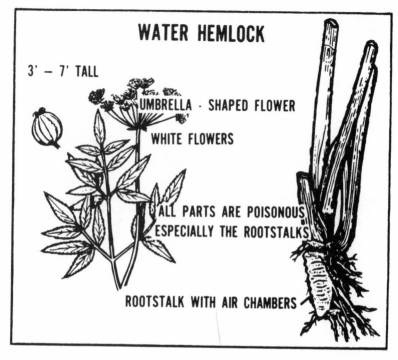

Figure 7-24. Poisonous Plants.

Cooking and discarding two changes of water lessen the amount of poisonous material or remove it completely. These boiling periods should last at least 5 minutes each.

(d) Place approximately one teaspoon of the prepared plant food in the mouth and chew it but do not swallow it.

1. If unpleasant effects occur (burning, bitter, or nauseating taste, etc.), remove the material from the mouth at once and discard that plant as a food source.

2. If no unpleasant effects occur, swallow the plant material and wait 8 hours.

(e) If after 8 hours, no unpleasant effects have occurred (nausea, cramps, diarrhea, etc.), eat about two tablespoonfuls and wait 8 hours.

(f) If no unpleasant effects have occurred at the end of this 8-hour period, the plant may be considered edible.

(g) Keep in mind that any new or strange food should be eaten with restraint until the body system has become accustomed to it.

(h) Plants selected by exceptions to the above system should be used as a food source only when positive identification can be made.

(i) The flowering portions of practically all plants are edible. Care must be exercised in removing only the flowering portion.

7-3. Preparation of Foods:

a. Animal food will give the greatest food value per pound.

   (1) Butchering and skinning:

      (a) Remove the skin.

         1. Glove skinning (figure 7-25).

         2. One cut skinning of small game (figure 7-26).

   (b) Open abdominal cavity carefully to avoid the rupture of intestines.

   (c) Remove the intestines.

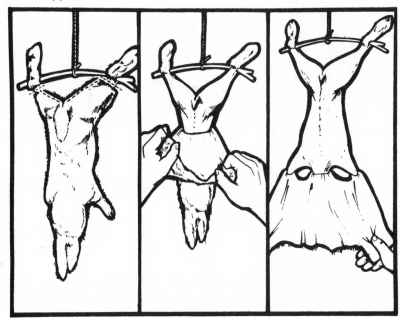

Figure 7-25. Glove Skinning.

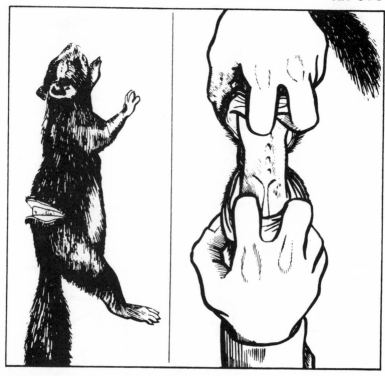

Figure 7-26. Small Game Skinning.

(d) Save inner organs (heart, liver, kidneys) and all meaty parts of the skull—the brains, tongue and eyes.

CAUTION: Discard all internal organs if liver or other organs are spotted.

(e) Wash when ready to use.

(f) If the meat is to be preserved, remove it from the bones.

(g) Skin all frogs and snakes (discard skin, head, and internal organs).

(2) Cleaning fish (scale and gut fish soon after procurement):

(a) Scale fish if necessary.

(b) Insert knife point into anus of fish and cut open the belly.

(c) Remove entrails.

(d) Remove gills to prevent spoilage.

(3) Birds:

(a) Gut birds soon after they are killed and protect them from flies.

(b) You may skin or pluck birds.

(c) Scavengers and sea birds should be skinned.

(4) Insects. Remove all hard portions such as the legs of grasshoppers or crickets. The rest is edible. Recommend cooking grasshopper-size insects.

b. Cooking:

(1) All wild game, freshwater fish, clams, mussels, snails, crawfish, and scavenger birds must be thoroughly cooked to kill internal parasites. Saltwater fish may be eaten raw.

(2) Boiling is the most nutritious method of cooking as long as the broth is consumed.

(a) Metal cooking containers can be made from ration cans.

(b) Heated rocks can be dropped into flammable containers to boil water or cook food.

(3) Baking:

(a) Wrap in leaves or pack in mud.

(b) Bury food in dirt under coals of fire.

(4) Fruits, berries, and most nuts can be eaten raw.

(a) Some nuts (acorns) must be leached to remove the bitter taste of tanin.

   1. Leaching:

      a. Soaking and pouring the water off.

      b. Crushing and pouring water through. Cold water should be tried first; however, boiling water is sometimes best.

      c. Discard water.

   2. Another method is:

      a. Boil, pour off water, and taste the plant.

      b. If bitter, repeat process until palatable.

(b) Shelled nuts may be roasted by shaking with hot coals.

7-4. Preservation of Foods:

a. Keeping an animal alive is one method of preserving it.

b. Refrigeration:

(1) Food buried in snow will maintain a temperature of approximately 32° F.

(2) Food wrapped in waterproof material and placed in a stream will remain cool in summer months.

(3) Earth below the surface, particularly in shady areas or along streams, remains cooler than the surface.

(4) When water evaporates, it tends to cool the surrounding area. Articles of food may be wrapped in absorbent material such as cotton and rewetted as the water evaporates.

c. Once food is frozen, it will not decompose. Freeze in meal-size portions.

d. Drying (sun or smoke) removes moisture and preserves food.
   (1) Smoking (figure 7-27).
      (a) Use salt, if available, to improve flavor and promote drying.
      (b) *Do not use* pitch woods such as fir or pine as they produce soot and give the meat an undesirable taste.
   (2) Sun drying (figure 7-28). Use the same techniques as in smoking.

e. Protecting meat from animals and insects:
   (1) How to wrap food:
      (a) Use clean parachute or other suitable material.

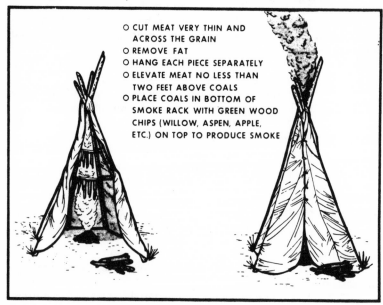

○ CUT MEAT VERY THIN AND ACROSS THE GRAIN
○ REMOVE FAT
○ HANG EACH PIECE SEPARATELY
○ ELEVATE MEAT NO LESS THAN TWO FEET ABOVE COALS
○ PLACE COALS IN BOTTOM OF SMOKE RACK WITH GREEN WOOD CHIPS (WILLOW, ASPEN, APPLE, ETC.) ON TOP TO PRODUCE SMOKE

Figure 7-27. Smoking.

Figure 7-28. Sun Drying.

    (b) Wrap pieces individually.

    (c) Assure all corners of the wrapping are insect proof.

  (2) Hanging meat:

    (a) Cover during daylight hours to protect from insects.

    (b) Hang meat in the shade.

  (3) Packing meat on the trail:

    (a) Wrap it before flies appear in the morning.

    (b) Roll packages of meat in fabric or clothing to form insulation.

    (c) Place the meat inside the pack for carrying. Soft material acts as insulation and helps keep the meat cool.

    (d) Carry shellfish, crabs, and shimp in wet seaweed.

  f. Preservation of plant foods:

    (1) Same as animal.

    (2) Soft fruits and berries can be wrapped in leaves or moss.

  g. Food should not be stored in the shelter as it may attract unwanted animal life.

Chapter 8

INDUCED CONDITIONS

(NUCLEAR, BIOLOGICAL, AND CHEMICAL)

8-1. Nuclear Conditions:
  a. Protection:
   (1) Gather parachute and survival kit.
   (2) Avoid detection and capture.

Figure 8-1. Immediate Action Shelter.

   (3) Find protective shelter within 5 minutes.
      (a) Seek existing shelter which may be improved (figure 8-1).
      (b) If no shelter is available, dig a trench or foxhole.
         1. Dig trench deep enough to obtain protection, then enlarge for comfort (figure 8-2).
         2. Cover with available material (figure 8-3).
   (4) Leave contaminated equipment and clothing near shelter for retrieval after radioactive decay.
   (5) Decontaminate body, clothing, and equipment.

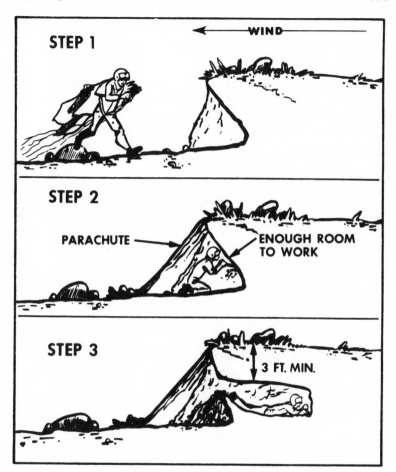

Figure 8-2. Improvised Shelter.

     (a) Wash with soap and water, if available, without leaving shelter.

     (b) If water is not available, exposed skin should be wiped with soft material to remove contaminated dust and dirt.

     (6) Lie down, keep warm, sleep, and rest.

     (7) Stay in complete isolation from 4 to 6 days following delivery of last weapon.

ONE THICKNESS REDUCES RECEIVED RADIATION DOSE BY ONE-HALF.
ADDITIONAL THICKNESS ADDED TO ANY AMOUNT OF THICKNESS REDUCES
RECEIVED RADIATION DOSE BY ONE-HALF.

IRON/STEEL	0.7 IN	EARTH	3.3 IN	WOOD (SOFT)	8.8 IN
BRICK	2.0 IN	CINDER BLOCK	5.3 IN	SNOW	20.3 IN
CONCRETE	2.2 IN	ICE	6.8 IN		

Figure 8-3. Radiation Shielding Efficiencies.

(a) On 7th day, one exposure of not more than 30 minutes.

(b) On 8th day, one exposure of not more than 1 hour.

(c) From 9th day through the 12th day, exposure of 2 to 4 hours per day.

(8) Normal operation may be resumed after 2 weeks.

b. Sustenance:

(1) Water:

(a) Allow no more than 30 minutes exposure on 3d day for water procurement.

(b) Water sources (in order of preference):

1. Springs, wells, or other underground sources - safest.

2. Water in pipes or containers in abandoned buildings.

3. Snow six or more inches below the surface during the fallout.

4. Streams and rivers - water should be filtered before drinking.

5. Lakes, ponds, pools, etc.

a. Water should be taken from just below the surface, taking care not to stir up the water.

b. Use a seep well.

(c) Water preparation:

1. Filtering through earth removes 99% of radioactivity (figure 8-4).

2. Purify all water sources.

(2) Food:

(a) Processed foods (canned or packaged) are preferred. Wash and wipe containers before use.

(b) Animal foods (figure 8-5):

1. Avoid animals which appear to be sick.

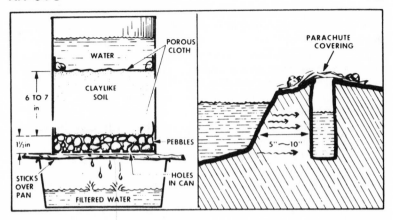

Figure 8-4. Filtration Systems.

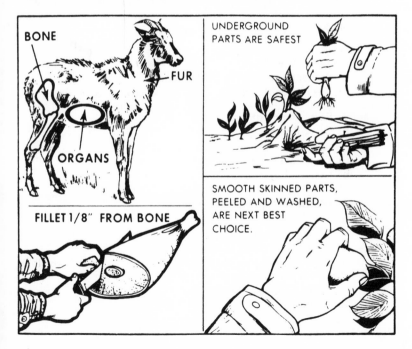

Figure 8-5. Food Procurement.

  2. Skin carefully to avoid radioactive particles contaminating the meat.

  3. Before cooking, cut meat away from the bone, leaving at least ⅛ inch of meat on the bone.

  4. Discard all internal organs.

  5. Cook all meat until very well done.

 (c) Avoid:

  1. Aquatic food sources; may be used only in extreme emergencies due to high concentration of radiation.

  2. Shells of all eggs; contents will be safe to eat.

  3. Milk from animals.

 (d) Plant foods (in order of preference):

  1. Plants whose edible portions grow underground (for example, potatoes, turnips, carrots, etc.). Wash and remove skin.

  2. Edible portions growing above ground which can be washed and peeled or skinned (for example, bananas, apples, etc.).

  3. Smooth skinned vegetables, fruits, or above ground plants, which are not easily peeled or washed.

 c. Self-aid:

  (1) General rules:

   (a) Prevent exposure to contaminants.

   (b) Use personal hygiene practices and remove body waste from shelter.

   (c) Rest; avoid fatigue.

   (d) Drink liquids.

  (2) Wounds:

   (a) Clean affected area.

   (b) Use antibacterial ointment or cleaning solution.

   (c) Cover with clean dressing.

   (d) Watch for signs of infection.

  (3) Burns:

   (a) Clean affected area.

   (b) Cover with clean dressing.

  (4) Radiation sickness (nausea, weakness, fatigue, vomiting, diarrhea, loss of hair, radiation burns).

   (a) Takes time to overcome.

   (b) Rest.

   (c) Drink fluids.

   (d) Take antivomiting agent.

   (e) Maintain food intake.

   (f) Prevent additional exposure.

8-2. Biological Conditions:

a. Clues which may alert you to a biological attack:

(1) Enemy aircraft dropping objects or spraying.

(2) Breakable containers or unusual types of bombs, particularly those which burst with little or no blast.

(3) Smoke or mist of unknown origin.

(4) Unusual substances on the ground or on vegetation; sick looking plants or crops.

b. Protection from biological agents:

(1) Use protective equipment.

(2) Bathe as soon as the situation permits.

(3) Wash hair and body thoroughly with soap (if available) and water.

(4) Clean thoroughly under fingernails.

(5) Clean teeth, gums, tongue, and roof of mouth frequently.

c. Survival tips for biological conditions:

(1) Keep your body and living area clean.

(2) Stay alert for signs of biological attack.

(3) Keep nose, mouth, and skin covered.

(4) Keep food and water protected. Bottled or canned foods are safe if sealed. If in doubt, boil food and water for 10 minutes.

(5) Construct shelter in a clear area, away from vegetation, with entrance 90° to the prevailing wind.

(6) If traveling, travel crosswind or upwind (taking advantage of weather to stay away from depressions).

8-3. Chemical Conditions:

a. Detecting:

(1) Smell—many agents have little or no odor.

(2) Sight:

(a) Color—yellow, orange, or red smoke or mist.

(b) Liquid—oily, dark patches on leaves, ground, etc. (figure 8-6).

(c) Gas—some agents may appear as a mist immediately after shell burst.

(d) Solid—most solid state agents have some color.

(3) Hearing—muffled explosions are possible indications of chemical agent bombs.

Figure 8-6. Detecting Chemical Agents.

(4) Feel—irritation to the nose, eyes, or skin and (or) moisture on the skin are danger signs.

(5) Taste—strange taste in food or water indicates contamination.

(6) General indications—tears, difficult breathing, choking, itching, coughing, dizziness.

b. Protection against chemical agents:

(1) Use protective equipment.

(2) Avoid contaminated areas.

(a) Exit contaminated area by moving crosswind.

(b) Select routes on high ground.

(c) Avoid cellars, ditches, trenches, gullies, valleys, etc.

(d) Avoid woods, tall grasses, and bushes as they tend to hold chemical agent vapors.

(e) Decontaminate body and equipment as soon as possible:

1. Removing—pinch-blotting.

2. Neutralizing—warm water.

3. Destroying—burying.

c. Self-aid in chemically contaminated areas:

(1) If a chemical defense ensemble is available:

(a) Use all protective equipment.

(b) Follow antidote directions.

(2) If a chemical defense ensemble is not available:

(a) Remove or tear away contaminated clothing.

(b) Rinse contaminated areas with water.

(c) Use antidote only when needed.

d. Tips for the survivor:

(1) Do not use wood from a contaminated area for fire.

(2) Look for signs of chemical agents around water sources prior to procurement (oil spots, foreign odors, dead fish or animals).

(3) Keep food and water protected.

(4) Do not use plants for food or water in contaminated area.

BY ORDER OF THE SECRETARY OF THE AIR FORCE

OFFICIAL

CHARLES A. GABRIEL, General, USAF
Chief of Staff

JAMES H. DELANEY, Colonel, USAF
Director of Administration

SUMMARY OF CHANGES

This revision contains a new outline format. New material has been added for evasion, chemical, and biological conditions. Text and illustrations are updated and corrected throughout.

SPIRITUAL SURVIVAL CHECKLIST

1. After Landing:

a. Remember you are not alone—God is there.

b. Pray for God's help, strength, wisdom, and rescue.

c. If you can remember scripture verses or hymns, repeat them to yourself or to God

2. At Hole-Up Site:

a. Worship without aid of written scripture or liturgies and without clergy or other people.
- (1) Try to remember scriptures—meditate:
    - (a) Lord's Prayer; Sh'ma.
    - (b) 23d Psalm.
- (2) Pray—talk to God:
    - (a) Thank God that He is with you.
    - (b) Ask for God's help.
- (3) Hymns and songs—sing to God and yourself:
    - (a) Church and religious hymns.
    - (b) Patriotic songs.
- (4) Portions of liturgy—repeat to God and self:
    - (a) Psalms, creeds, or communion words.
    - (b) Pledge of Allegiance.

b. Forgive:
- (1) Those who have failed you.
- (2) Yourself for what you have done or said that was wrong.

c. Praise and thanks:
- (1) Thank God that He is bigger than your circumstances.
- (2) Rejoice that no matter what happens He will see you through.
- (3) Faith in America.
- (4) For leaders—President—commanders.
- (5) For heaven or eternal life.

d. Trust:
- (1) Faith in God and friends.
- (2) Love for family and self.
- (3) Hope—never lose hope—never give up.

3. With Other Survivors:

  a. Pray for each other.
  b. Share scriptures and songs.
  c. Appoint a chaplain.
  d. Try to have short worship services.
  e. Write down scriptures, songs, or liturgies that are remembered.
  f. Encourage each other while waiting for rescue:
    (1) God loves you.
    (2) Praise the Lord.